SECOND EDITION

D1545526

SPECIAL EVENTS

Planning for Success

BY APRIL L. HARRIS

CASE®

ISBN-10: 0-89964-333-7
ISBN-13: 978-0-89964-333-5

Printed in United States of America

1st edition, 1988
reprinted 1990 and 1995
2nd edition, 1998
reprinted 2005
reprinted 2015

Council for Advancement and Support of Education (CASE) is the international education association serving professionals in the disciplines of alumni relations, communications, and philanthropy.

CASE offers high-quality training, information resources, and a wide variety of books, videotapes, and materials for advancement professionals.

For more information on CASE or a copy of our product catalog, visit our website *www.case.org* or call (202) 328-2273.

Book design: Fletcher Design
Editor: Cathryn Seymour Dorsey

Council for Advancement and Support of Education
1307 New York Avenue, NW
Suite 1000
Washington, DC 20005-4701

Table of Contents

Foreword

TO ESTABLISH BROAD AWARENESS OF OUR institutions, we rely largely on the printed word, an impersonal medium. Yet, to secure commitments, we realize that face-to-face interchange is crucial. For example, our first contact with a prospective student is often the aptly named "search piece." It is usually brief in length and broad in content, a general advertisement for our institution. Yet, experience teaches us that a student is not likely to enroll on the strength of captivating publications alone. The decision usually comes after a campus visit or the personal encouragement of a current student or an alumnus. By the same token, a donor may first become intrigued with our institution by an article in the alumni magazine. We know, however, that he or she is not likely to give a significant gift without a personal attention from some senior official. The process of persuasion begins with general and impersonal forms of communication and culminates in highly focused, eye-to-eye appeals.

In that light, consider the enormous importance of special events. For donors, community leaders, students, elected officials and many others, special events can represent a turning point in their decision-making. For many, a special event may constitute their first personal contact with our institution. An event could be the catalyst for transforming a visitor's abstract interest into tangible appreciation. The well-planned and well-executed event can convert a fence-sitter into an advocate or a passive board member into an active one. Events can make vague concepts come to life or help instill pride. On the other hand, weak events can discourage constituents from wanting to learn more, if not drive them away altogether. One way or the other, special events represent critical junctures in the persuasion process.

Yet, too often, special events have been treated like frills. Events coordinators are not always seen as key members of a strategic planning team. Even senior advancement officers have treated special events as independent, unrelated events, not as crucial steps in constituent development efforts. We recognize the need for a "family look" to unify our publications but rarely insist that our events reflect the same discipline and continuity of purpose.

This book, then, represents an important part of the institutional advancement library. Its presence elevates the importance of special events in our strategic thinking and its contents deliver a wealth of practical experience. Even the most seasoned events specialist will benefit from its comprehensive checklists, useful tips, and cautionary tales. However, I hope this book finds it way to the shelves of communications strategists, development officers, student recruiters, marketing mavens, and senior advancement officers. Its place there will remind us of one of the eternal verities of communication. That verity was impressed on me many moons ago by a crusty editor. Having grown weary of my penchant for adjectives and metaphors, he scribbled in the margin, “Show, don’t tell!”

There are lots of ways you can tell people about your institutional strengths and aspirations. Special events may be the best way to show them. This book won't tell you how to incorporate events into your advancement plans. That's up to you. But it will show you how to plan and execute a truly special event.

James M. Langley
Vice Chancellor
External Relations
University of California at San Diego

Preface

A LARGE PAIR OF SCISSORS WIELDED BY A man in a sweatsuit flashed in the stage lights as the popular television personality we'd hired to emcee the Athletic Hall of Fame Induction directed his attention to the script I had sent him weeks before. It was obvious this was the first time he had read it. It wasn't his style. "Trust me," he said, slicing away, "I'll improvise."

He had been a no-show for that afternoon's rehearsal. I'd burned an entire cellular phone battery trying to track him down. Thirty minutes before show time he blew into the ballroom and was now cutting 15 pages of script into little shreds while shouting questions to me about the order of the evening. I wondered if he had remembered to bring his tuxedo.

Behind me, the waiters were pouring water into the guests' glasses and the candles were being lit. In moments the doors would open on this distinguished event. We had been sold out for weeks. Every VIP in the state, a star-studded cast of former professional and Olympic athletes, and 500 paying guests were munching hors d'oeuvres on the other side of the ballroom doors. Little did they know the evening's program had just been reduced to strips of paper. I prayed they would never realize they were being led by a man who had never seen the video he was about to narrate, had never practiced pronouncing the inductees' names, and didn't know any of them by sight.

The pianist was awaiting his cue; dinner was ready. The time had come to tell this guy to scoop up the scraps and go get dressed. Like a daredevil who realizes too late that luck has finally run out, I sensed a career-ending catastrophe. No way could we pull this off. Transfixed by the flashing scissors, I stood glued to the spot, heart pounding, wearing my little black dress and proper pearls, struggling to remember, compress, and tell him everything he needed to know in a precious few minutes. I never dreamed it would end like this. . . . If I live though this night, I'll never do another event. . . .

INTRODUCTION

So You're Thinking of Holding a Special Event

SPECIAL EVENTS ARE THOSE OCCASIONS TO which an institution invites outsiders—whether they are alumni, business leaders, parents, donor prospects, potential students, or even members of one department visiting another—for a closer, more personalized look at the facilities, faculty, staff, students, and policies of an institution than is generally afforded on a daily basis.

Special events can include annual events, such as homecoming, commencement, convocations, retirement recognitions, and parents' day. They can be unique, one-time events, like the dedication of a new facility, the celebration of an anniversary, or the inauguration of a president. Or they can be events planned specifically for a certain audience, such as donor recognition, legislative relations days, or academic symposia.

Special events can also take place away from your campus. These might include conferences and workshops, planning retreats, alumni meetings in faraway cities, or alumni days at places like a museum, a major-league ball game, an amusement park, or an off-campus restaurant or hotel.

Sometimes, major special events have many small events tucked under the umbrella of a large theme. On a convocation day, subevents might include a hospitality reception for the press, a breakfast for visiting dignitaries, a morning program, special displays and tours, a luncheon, a post-convocation reception in a tent for special guests, and a private dinner with the president that evening for a few select individuals.

Whether an event is massive in scope and available to the general public, like a concert, or private, such as dinner for five key alumni at the president's home, special events put an institution on display. They offer the opportunity for people to look at and, indeed, to scrutinize the institution and its programs. Powerful communicators, special events send messages that make a far more lasting impression than the most expensive brochure or the slickest alumni magazine money can buy.

Because special events are such powerful communication tools, be sure to use them wisely: Never lose sight of the long-range goals of your advancement program. Do not create your special events in isolation but weave them into your total program so that all activities complement each other.

Each event must be consistent with the spirit and tone of your advancement program and the institutional image you want to communicate to your friends. The most brilliantly designed and executed special event will be counterproductive if its message is confusing or inconsistent with your institution's other activities. Plan and implement your special events so that they will add to and not detract from the central themes of your institution.

Special events are akin to inviting guests to your home for dinner. In the same way a dinner guest can gather information about your financial status, eating and drinking habits, reading preferences, and approaches to childrearing, guests at special events can draw conclusions about your institution. Special events reveal more in a few hours' time about institutional priorities, politics, financial condition, management style, and needs than a year's worth of news releases or magazine articles.

Because their impact is so forceful, because they cover the spectrum from routine to stupendous, and because they are planned and managed by everyone from admissions officers to university relations personnel to volunteers and committees, it is important to understand the role of special events in the institution's overall advancement plan and realize what special events can and cannot accomplish.

A well-planned special event begins with that old journalistic formula, "who, what, when, where, how, why" (and as a professor of mine added, "so what?"). Successful events are rooted in thoughtful, sometimes frustrating planning. You may be tempted to build a grand event full of razzle-dazzle and hoopla, but if it is not solidly anchored in mission-accomplishing strategy, your efforts—and money—will be wasted.

There is one valid reason to sponsor a special event: It supports and enhances institutional goals and mission, contributing to the accomplishment of objectives in academics, alumni relations, fund raising, student recruitment, or image building. Random events held for the sake of a one-day success or as a diversion from daily routine can send mixed messages to your audiences and sap resources that could be used more effectively in a well-planned public relations program.

Therefore, before agreeing to plan and hold a special event, ask yourself these questions. Does the event

- support the institution's mission,
- help achieve specific goals,
- showcase resources unique to your institution,
- help raise friends or funds,
- build goodwill,
- consistently comply with the institutional image, and
- match available resources?

If the answer to any of these questions is no, send the idea to the scrap heap and review the conditions that gave rise to it. Ask yourself: Why do we think we need a special event? What do we hope to accomplish? Is a special event the most effective tool to fill the need?

Special events ideas that pass the test can yield powerful minutes of undivided attention from your target audiences. A potent "show and tell," special events provide the opportunity to deliver your message personally to your constituents by showcasing your institution in interesting, time-effective, creative ways.

Special events can help you educate, make a point, build friendships, enable your constituents to feel like "insiders," and foster a sense of community. Last but not least, special events are enjoyable, pleasant means of social interaction.

There are several things special events cannot accomplish no matter how well planned they might be. Special events cannot erase years of neglect; they cannot instantly turn the tide of an institution's image or act as a Band-Aid to cover up bad policies or poor leadership.

Instead, like a holiday, special events serve to bring resources, people, and messages together to accomplish specific objectives. With proper research, planning, communications, and implementation, special events can be some of the most effective, creative, and enjoyable components of a comprehensive institutional advancement plan.

CHAPTER 1

Plan Ahead

PLANNING IS THE MOST CRUCIAL, MOST time-consuming aspect of successful special events. This chapter focuses on planning at the conceptual level—how the event will fit into and contribute to your total institutional advancement efforts. The balance of this book explores planning at the concrete level—the mass of painstaking details that are necessary to produce a successful special event.

Special events should be developed in the context of your institution's annual public relations plan and in relation to long-range institutional advancement goals. Positioning special events in a master plan helps avoid duplication of effort and waste of money. It prevents you from bombarding the same target audience with too many messages and too many invitations. Good planning can help you piggyback on other communication efforts for more meaningful impact. Master planning also helps ensure that events are consistent with institutional goals in public relations, image building, and marketing.

Let's say that one of your most prominent alumni is the head of a national scientific research organization. He recently has been the focus of media attention and has offered to speak at your campus at no cost to your institution. The construction of the new chemistry building on campus is nearing completion, and the ribbon-cutting will take place sometime this year. By timing his visit to coincide with the ribbon-cutting, you can draw more attention to this talk, guarantee a better crowd, and add a bit of sparkle to what could otherwise be a routine dedication ceremony.

Sound easy? It's not. Perhaps the chemistry department has already selected a speaker. Perhaps the planners of the ribbon-cutting will resent your office butting in on their event. Perhaps the alumnus is not held in high regard by the chemistry faculty. Perhaps he doesn't want to be the focus of more publicity.

The point is, never assume anything. An idea that looks great at first blush may not appear so when viewed in relation to the big picture. Only through one-on-one discussions with other campus event planners can you make sense of the big picture and put together a special events calendar that will pack a wallop and return the greatest public relations payoff.

Guided in the long term by the institutional mission and in the short term by institutional goals and objectives, the central university relations office (or its counterpart on your campus) should serve as a clearinghouse for all special events. That is, any time you are considering sponsoring an event designed to attract outside attention, from the media, alumni, or the general public, the chief university relations officer should be consulted before ideas become plans.

From a purely textbook point of view, all special events should be managed from a central office, and today, many larger institutions are creating special events offices for this purpose. In reality, many institutions are too large and too sparsely staffed to take on such a task. Instead, planners are scattered across campus assigned to specific departments. Nevertheless, one person, such as the chief PR or university relations officer should have the final approval on all major special events, particularly if they involve politicians, celebrities, or controversial speakers or topics or encompass a university-wide celebration such as an anniversary.

• • •

Do It by Campus Committee

Often, you can learn more about what is happening on your campus by reading the newspaper than you can at work. It is very common for campus departments to work in isolation, resulting in missed opportunities to partner on events or, worse yet, in parallel events. At one university, the athletic department and the library planned fund-raising auctions within two weeks of each other. Both used the same facility and the same volunteer auctioneer, requested donations from the same businesses, and invited essentially the same guest list. Both auctions' fund-raising totals suffered. Guests wondered aloud at the similarities between the two events. The planners were embarrassed. The situation could have been avoided by assembling a committee of people on campus who plan special events. The purpose of such a group is to learn what others are doing, consider the list of proposed events, weed out the marginal ones, and schedule the remaining events to avoid duplication, build impact, and maximize the investment of time and money.

A good time for this committee to meet is at the start of the academic year. The first meeting should be very general with the chief university relations officer providing an overview of priorities and goals for the coming year. He or she should sketch the framework of major projects—such as a building dedication, fund drive, the visit of international dignitaries—within which the committee can plan the year's events.

This is the time to talk about the programs, people, and projects that need to be highlighted. It is the time to confirm the dates for major functions, such as commencements, concerts, parents' day, and sports events. It is also an opportunity to gather information that can avert event-planning disasters—such as scheduling a large event at the student union during the time its parking lot will be closed for resurfacing, or planning a scholarship fund-raising concert on the same night that your campus will host the ice hockey championships.

• • •

Your Master Plan

Armed with a sense of the big picture for the coming year, you can then develop your own office-wide special events master plan. Work your plans around the events already in place. This may mean avoiding a date, dovetailing into a date, or just being aware of other activities and how they could affect availability of space, services, media coverage, and your targeted participants.

Refer to the written goals and objectives for your office. What do you want to accomplish? What are the timetables and deadlines?

A good tool to use for this planning exercise is a wall calendar that displays the entire year. Block in the events already scheduled—homecoming, commencements, board meetings, and breaks. Study the calendar. Are several events crowded into a few consecutive weeks? Are they intended for the same audience? Will major events already on the calendar prevent you from having access to a facility or service you need?

Referring to your goals and objectives, make a list of what needs to be accomplished; leave the "how" until later in the planning process. For example, if you are a member of the development staff, your "what" list might include twice-a-year contact with faculty emeriti, major donor recognition, an announcement for the wrap up of a successful fund drive, contact with parents of scholarship students, and recognition of volunteers who have helped with fund raising throughout the year.

In the public affairs office, your "what" list might contain items such as introducing the president to community business leaders and area media, making key legislators more aware of funding needs, recognizing student leaders, and planning the annual convocation.

Now, match goals and objectives with key dates whenever possible, and, considering your "what needs to be accomplished" list, look for logical tie-ins for your target audiences. For example, you know that the School of Music will sponsor a concert series beginning in February. The afternoon preceding the first concert may be the perfect time to invite select donor prospects to a dinner and present plans to enhance the concert hall.

Pencil in dates that seem attractive: consider the availability of staff and facilities, especially on weekends that are already busy. Will there be enough time to prepare facilities, or are events stacked back-to-back so that one delay means disaster for all that follow? Will your staff be spread too thinly to handle the work effectively? Are so many events planned that caterers and service personnel will be in short supply?

Think about the people you want to involve. Will they have just been to campus for another event? For example, if you plan a recent-graduate reunion within a few weeks of homecoming, alumni will probably choose one event or the other but not both. By moving your recent-graduate reunion to a spring weekend, you stand a better chance of having solid attendance at both functions. Or you could package the two events on the same weekend, thereby increasing the incentive for alumni to attend.

Next, get specific. You've analyzed the big picture; you've zeroed in on probable dates. What should you plan? Think about each project's significance as part of your total master plan and how it will fulfill the specific goals you've decided upon. At this point, you should decide whether or not to use a committee to develop plans and how much leeway such a committee would have.

• • •

Principles to Live By

Follow a few basic principles when you are deciding on the theme or type of event your institution will sponsor.

Consider the target audiences. Are they young, old, students, professionals? Are they alumni or parents who are familiar with your campus, or are they people who have never been on campus before? Are they affluent or on a shoestring budget? Are they members of a constituency that will have several opportunities to participate in events on your campus during the year, or are they a group for which this special event may be the only firsthand exposure for several years?

Be certain the event is consistent with your institution's image and principles. For example, if alcoholic beverages are not permitted on campus, don't try to skirt the rule in an attempt to incorporate them into an event. Don't merely work within your limitations, but use them to make a positive statement about your support of your institution's rules and principles.

A national health organization specializing in educating the public about good nutrition and prevention of heart disease sponsored a star-studded fund-raising gala. The dinner guests were served a high-fat meal of meats, sauces, and desserts that the organization advises people to avoid. Why did the organization's planners choose such a menu? Because they were afraid paying guests would not feel they had received their money's worth if a low-fat dinner was served.

What a public relations opportunity they missed! The planners should have worked with the situation, instead of against it, to wow their guests with a menu featuring the healthier foods that the organization advocates. They could have designed a menu card that compared the nutritional value of each item to that of standard banquet fare. They could have created a model—and delicious—meal that would encourage their guests to make healthful choices in daily life.

Use events to highlight features unique to your institution. Or, at the very least, focus on attractions that are not readily available elsewhere in your community. Draw attention to the programs, people, and facilities that set your institution apart. You will increase attendance at your event and make a long-lasting impression on the people you invite.

• • •

Events' Role in Fund Raising

Special events play two main roles in fund raising—cultivation or "friend raising" and making money through the sale of tickets or other means. It can sometimes be difficult to define where friend raising stops and fund raising starts. Both types of events are part of a comprehensive development plan to support institutional fund-raising activities and, as such, become intertwined. While guests at a black-tie dinner to launch a capital campaign may not be asked for contributions that night, they understand that the request is inevitable. Is the event a friend raiser or a fund raiser?

On some campuses, glamorous events for which guests pay high prices are the focal points of the fund-raising year. Other institutions never charge current or prospective donors for any event, regardless of how elaborate it is.

A solid college or university development program cannot rely exclusively on special events to meet its fund-raising goals any more than friend-raising events can meet goals without proper development follow-up. Whatever the present mix of friend-raising and fund-raising events on your campus, finding the right balance is the key to success.

In finding that balance, you should select events that make the maximum impact on your target audience by using the same formula that is applied to selecting other events. Fund-raising events must be consistent with your institution's image, help to achieve specific goals, showcase resources that are unique to your institution, build goodwill, and match available resources. And remember that all events must have an action follow-up. People want and need to know what you want them to do next. What should they expect? Is a development officer going to call? Will a pledge card arrive by mail? Do you want them to volunteer their time?

Events aren't new to fund raising; they have been around for a very long time. In days gone by, large fund-raising events called "benefits" or "galas" were, for the most part, the exclusive domain of arts organizations. Today, many fund-raising events jam the social calendars of universities and the communities in which they reside, making it increasingly difficult to find interesting, relevant events that will raise a significant amount of money. Such a crowded field is also hard on the people who are invited. These days, it's difficult to find anyone of means who hasn't already been invited to several charitable fund-raising events this year. These are important reasons to be certain the fund-raising events you sponsor carry a message, are directly related to supporting your role and mission, and make sense in terms of the big picture on your campus.

• • •

Prune the Deadwood

Planning time is also an excellent opportunity to take a critical look at annual events that have been on the calendar for a number of years. As the years pass, the events schedule can become cluttered with receptions and the like for which the purpose is long forgotten or the effectiveness has been diminished by the passing of time. These events consume resources like money and staff time that perhaps could be used more effectively elsewhere.

Before automatically rescheduling everything that was done last year, analyze each event's purpose and audience and determine if it is the most effective use of time and money. Many events can be quietly dropped, consolidated with others, or updated. So doing helps keep the events schedule efficient and fresh. But use caution before making arbitrary cuts. One planner recalls as the worst time of her career the furor she created by eliminating what she saw as an inefficient, stale event that had been on the schedule for years.

• • •

Be Prepared to Say No

From time to time, ideas will surface (especially when working with committees) that are not in sync with your institution's image or that would use up most (or all) of your budget. Unfortunately, these are often the ideas that really catch on and inspire their originators to dig in and begin working.

Whether you are responsible for institutional relations as a whole, or just for the events of a particular department, if the idea is not consistent with the special-events master plan, it is your obligation to speak up and quash it. Do this in a constructive way, armed with alternative suggestions as well as a well-thought-out explanation of your master plan.

If a committee is involved, it may help to quietly enlist support for your point of view with an influential member and have him or her present the alternative.

• • •

Financing: How to Pay for Special Events

By their very nature, special events fall outside of the traditional budgeting process. Events can appear suddenly as an answer to a particular problem or as a way to take advantage of an unexpected opportunity. They can grow from modest to grand, seemingly overnight. The number and types of special events vary from year to year. One manager may be more resourceful than another in securing donations to underwrite special events. The projected cost of an event may fluctuate according to several different factors, from the size of the audience to the weather. Ticket sales may fall far short of projections, or you may discover that the decorating committee has overshot its budget by 50 percent. Budgeting for special events is therefore frequently a process of calculated, educated guesses.

Some planners have an annual budget allocation that includes seed money to invest in events that aim to be self-supporting or to underwrite part of the cost of certain events. They are the fortunate ones. More often than not, events are run on a no-budget basis, a concept that every planner is familiar with, but most business people find unimaginable.

Usually, staging a first-class event is a direct reflection of the planner's resourcefulness in borrowing equipment and supplies, making decorations out of available components (the recycled parts of another event's centerpieces), or appealing to donors or sponsors to supply needed elements. But while this is true, a seasoned planner also knows it is wise to build a preliminary budget based on facts and then decide where to add and subtract. Creating such a guideline is a good check to see if ideas are feasible and also helps prevent sticker shock caused by the arrival of unexpectedly large invoices after the event is over. It is preferable for everyone to know costs before plans go forward, rather than to discover far into the process that the ideas are lots more costly than imagined. People who don't make arrangements for food, entertainment, decor, or facilities frequently have no concept of how expensive these things can be. While it is good to have big plans and creative dreams, sooner or later the reality of funding must take over.

• • •

Build a Budget Based on Research

You should be able to build a budget proposal based on your master planning exercises. To do this, estimate the costs of each event, including

- facilities,
- equipment,
- security,
- entertainment,
- decorations,
- invitations and program printing,
- postage,
- food,
- extra help,
- speakers' fees,
- travel expenses, and
- liquor or wine.

Don't just guesstimate. Call local vendors to get estimates for each item or service. Shop around; you may find that some vendors can do certain things cheaper than their competitors.

Depending on the budget process at your institution, you may be able to acquire funding from several sources. Additional outside funding may be available from your alumni association or university foundation. Some universities, such as those receiving government money, cannot legally cover the costs of some types of special events, particularly if alcoholic beverages are served. Check with your institution's financial officer for any restrictions that may apply.

In fact, it's important to learn to work with your financial officer beforehand, so that you know the restrictions and procedures under which you must operate as well as the accounting and reporting procedures you must use to process your expenditures.

• • •

Find Corporate Sponsors

One way to underwrite the cost of a special event is to secure corporate or other private sponsorship. Since first coming on the scene in the 1980s, corporate sponsorships have grown into a multimillion-dollar business. An example of sponsorship on a large scale can be seen in the proliferation of corporate logos in the end zones of college football bowl games. Sponsorship is also heavily used by the arts and other charitable organizations that sponsor events for humanitarian or civic causes. Sponsorship can be highly visible and quite complicated or as simple as a company donating its products in exchange for public recognition. An example would be a local dairy supplying free ice cream for your fall freshman orientation.

Corporations are willing to make such gifts because they help build a positive public image and provide an entree to well-educated, affluent people who are not only potential consumers of corporate products but are also likely to be community opinion leaders.

Support for colleges and universities is attractive because these institutions produce the corporate personnel of the future, and it is good for the corporate image to be associated with higher education's traditional goals of teaching, research, and public service. Because most corporations give locally, sponsorship also helps build a vibrant, thriving community, creating an atmosphere that helps keep employees satisfied in their private lives and reduces employee turnover.

The bottom line is this: Corporations become event sponsors because it is good business. Therefore, package your request for sponsorship so that it clearly delineates the benefits to the corporation; strive to match the corporate interest and purpose with that of your own. For example, asking a pet food manufacturer to sponsor your veterinary college's dog show has a better chance of success than approaching a greeting card company with the same request. (Unless, of course, the card company is unveiling a new line of pet-related cards.)

Conversely, be sure the sponsor's image is one that will enhance your own. It is wise to avoid any association with products or groups that are controversial. Tobacco and alcohol products are two obvious examples.

While sponsorship can involve an outright gift of cash, corporations are more likely to sponsor a specific budget item such as the cost of food, invitations, or entertainment. For this reason, you may need several sponsors.

A word of caution: Never set out to secure corporate or foundation sponsorship of a special event without clearance from and coordination with your development office. This office may have a proposal pending before the potential sponsor. You don't want to endanger a larger, more important gift to your institution by not doing your homework. At the same time, you don't want other proposals coming in later and competing with yours.

The development office can save you from going down blind alleys, offer approaches to your potential sponsor that are based on experience in dealing with the organization, and possibly suggest alternative sources of support that you had not considered. Development professionals may also help you write a proposal or otherwise guide you in packaging a successful sales presentation.

Here are a few caveats of which you should be aware:

- Never assign joint sponsorship to any aspect of your event without the prior consent of the sponsors.
- Don't reproduce a corporate logo without permission.
- Don't promise tax deductions and giving recognition until you've checked with your development office. (Not all gifts qualify for a tax deduction.)
- If you are dealing with athletic events, be certain sponsor agreements comply with the governing rules of the NCAA and any athletic conferences or leagues to which your institution belongs. This is especially important if the event you are planning is associated with an NCAA tournament.
- Be sure to give your sponsors full recognition in all printed matter concerning the event, e.g., on invitations, advertising, news releases, and, of course, at the event itself.

The rise of corporate sponsorship has led to numerous books and workshops on the subject and ingenious new ways to make these partnerships work.

• • •

Capitalize on Student Talent

Sometimes we overlook one of our most obvious and valuable resources: our students. Students in your school of music or theater can provide quality entertainment at little or no cost. One of our most successful dinners for our alumni association board of directors was planned, prepared, and served by students in the university's catering and restaurant management program. The board was so impressed that it voted to give the restaurant management program an annual scholarship appropriation.

The talents of art and theater students can be an invaluable source for event decor and lighting know-how. Computer and engineering students can likely wire some fabulous audiovisual effects and students in graphic design can create amazing invitations and printed materials.

By using students, you reduce overhead, give the students experience performing in a real-world setting, and enjoy the public relations advantage of showcasing the institution's number one product.

• • •

How to Use Planning Committees

Like it or not, the best events are those that are planned by committee. A well-managed committee provides the creativity of several people with varying points of view and differing ideas.

A good committee should include people who are active, involved, and well-informed about your institution and objectives. It should include representatives of each of the groups you are trying to reach. For example, a homecoming committee should include alumni, members of each reunion class, students, and faculty. Also include representatives of groups that will play a significant role in the success of the day, such as Greek organizations, the marching band, the athletic department, catering services, and campus security.

Well-chosen committee members can open doors for you. Enlist the participation of financial and social leaders, key business people, influential citizens, and prominent alumni. But don't select someone only for name or position. If an individual cannot make a specific contribution to the committee's mission, don't invite that person to serve. There may be an appropriate role on another project. You owe it to yourself, to the other committee members, and to your event to assemble the most active, creative, productive committee possible. By the same token, don't ask busy people to serve on a committee if you have no real intention of using their advice, talents, and time.

• • •

Working and Honorary Committees

There is a considerable difference between working committees and honorary committees. Members of a working committee are expected to do just that—roll up their sleeves, pitch in, and get the job done. Typically, members of this type of committee have similar professional and social status, although the chair may be a prominent alumnus, professional, or business leader.

Honorary committees (sometimes called advisory committees) may hold meetings but do not actually attend to details like selecting caterers or decorating the banquet hall. Honorary committees are usually composed of people with clout who give an event status with the target audience, and membership frequently is determined by social and economic prominence. This setup is common in campaign fund raising. An honorary or advisory committee may be assembled and listed on all campaign materials to give the cause stature. The group may never actually meet or perform any function. Sometimes advisory or honorary committee members may lend assistance by opening doors to possible large contributions, allowing their signatures to be used on fund-raising appeals, or meeting one-on-one with people in their areas. The committee's legwork is conducted behind the scenes by staff members.

When you are organizing an honorary committee, select a competent, polished staff member to act as assistant to the committee chair. This person should meet periodically with the chair to give a brief, well-organized progress report, determine the chair's wishes, and follow through accordingly. The staff member should be efficient but unobtrusive and ready to give full credit to the honorary chair who will bask in the limelight and serve as toastmaster on the evening of the successful event.

Although the buck always stops with paid staffers, this is especially true with honorary committees. Always follow up on suggestions and decisions made in committee meetings to be certain that action has really been taken. Check and double-check. Don't make the mistake of the staff member who discovered a few hours before a major banquet that the committee chair had not selected a menu as he had indicated he would!

• • •

How to Work with a Committee

A few basic guidelines will make working with committees easier and more productive.

- Establish a clear set of goals and objectives for the committee.
- Decide beforehand who will chair the committee and run each meeting. Selecting a person of stature to head your committee can open doors to your community's social world, give you political clout, and draw media attention to your project. The downside of this setup is you relinquish much of the control over the committee's management. Before the committee chair agrees to serve, he or she should be informed of the scope of the project, its budget limitations, and the level of commitment required in terms of time and financial resources.
- Regardless of who runs the meeting, make each session productive by distributing a written agenda and sticking to it. Whenever possible, mail a preliminary agenda to all committee members at least a week before the meeting is to be held.
- Take minutes of each meeting and distribute them. This will help keep the group on track and eliminate questions about who agreed to do what and when.
- The chair should wield a firm gavel, limit circuitous discussion and argument, and make clear assignments of specific tasks to committee members when no volunteers come forward.
- Committee meetings should begin on time, end on time, and not waste time in the middle.
- Respect your chair as a professional, and always be forthcoming with information related to the project.

• • •

Star Power: The Celebrity Special Event

Celebrities, authors, sports stars, and television personalities are always good draws for special events. Commencements are favorite times to invite celebrities to be featured speakers.

Celebrity events can serve as excellent fund-raising events and can be of incomparable significance in terms of public relations exposure for your institution, but they do come with their own special challenges, and they do require additional planning and expertise.

While hiring a big-name entertainer or other celebrity for an appearance may seem like an easy way to make money, you need skill and knowledge to negotiate contracts with agents, unions, and promoters; secure an appropriate facility; arrange technical needs such as sound, lights, and special staging; deal with security and liability insurance needs; and oversee an orderly ticket sale. You also need a hefty budget to invest in rental of a theater or an auditorium, to pay insurance premiums and deposits, to rent special equipment, and to make partial payments on contracts.

The advantage of hiring a celebrity is that entertainers can usually generate masses of good publicity, draw a large crowd easily, and raise a significant amount of money for a one-shot event.

Here are some fundamentals to consider:

- Know your audience and choose entertainment that will appeal to them. Chances are a rock group that the students love will not be a big hit in your Parents' Day show.
- Know the going rate for similar tickets in your area. Your show must be competitively priced to sell.
- Make sure that the same show will not be offered within easy driving distance of your campus for a minimum of one year before your date.
- Once the decision is made to sponsor a celebrity, select a number of people or acts that would be desirable in case your first choice is not available or is prohibitively expensive.
- Have all contracts reviewed by an attorney and figure the costs of extras stipulated in the contract rider before deciding whether you can afford it. Beware of hidden expenses such as advertising, ticket printing, expensive sound and lighting systems, and extra personnel.
- Begin the selection process at least a year in advance. Be prepared to negotiate, and keep negotiations confidential.

• • •

Working With Agents

To arrange a concert or performance by any prominent entertainer, you will have to negotiate with the entertainer's booking agent. Negotiations can take weeks or months and involve many minute changes to contracts and delays in finalizing deals. Sometimes an agent will put your negotiations on hold while he or she tries to put together more attractive dates in better places or larger cities. Occasionally an agent will abruptly end discussion on a contract that has been in the works for months. As you prepare to negotiate, it is helpful to remember that agents are paid by commission, usually 10 percent of the price for which they book a star. Obviously, an agent's main interest is keeping the price as high as possible.

Negotiations for talent may involve hidden costs that spell the difference between financial success and ruin for novice contract negotiators. Frequently, the price listed as the fee for the talent is only the tip of the iceberg. Costs that can really add up include requests for certain brands of musical instruments, specially constructed stages and lighting, first-class airline transportation, limousine service, special foods and beverages, and a host of other goods and services. One entertainer's contract stipulated that six quarts of whole milk be delivered to her room each day, not for her to drink but for her to bathe in! A rider on the contract of a male singer specified his suite be installed with a coal-black toilet, certified never to have been used. Obviously, all of these add-ons are negotiable. Protect yourself and prevent nasty surprise bills by stipulating in the contract that the celebrity is responsible for things like room service, meals for his or her entourage, and the expenses associated with rehearsals.

Occasionally celebrities will donate an appearance at little or no cost, usually because they will be in the area and have the time to do so, or because of a genuine belief in the sponsoring organization. But beware! You will still incur the costs of staging, lighting, paying for the backup band, and covering the expenses of the requirements listed in the person's usual contract rider. While "free" entertainment may save you thousands, it can still commit you to spending large amounts just to stage the show.

• • •

Hosting Dignitaries

When a high-level U.S. government official, a visiting head of state, or other dignitary is your guest or featured speaker, you will likely spend many hours dealing with an advance team. For some officials and candidates, you will also work with members of the Secret Service.

Advance teams travel from city to city making certain all preparations are in order before the arrival of the official. This advance team will take over virtually all aspects of the visit, from scheduling to reviewing menus to arranging security.

Typical of dignitary visits are requests to find obscure equipment and to achieve the seemingly impossible in a record amount of time.

One planner was asked by a presidential advance team to locate 14 matching coffee urns overnight—no easy task in a small Midwestern college town.

When the first lady visited a college campus in a small New York town, her team wanted a special type of dual microphone. Planners scoured the Northeast in vain trying to accommodate the demand. Because the request was made the same day the first lady arrived, a compromise was eventually reached that included covering a chrome-plated microphone with black tape to make it more visually pleasing. On another campus, hosts of a rally featuring the first lady politely declined her advance team's request to prune large branches from a stately old tree because it was covering the corner of a campaign sign.

When the Pope visited a U.S. campus, the grounds crew removed light poles that interfered with camera angles, painted a yellow fire hydrant green so that it would blend in with the grass, and vacuumed the lawn just before his helicopter touched down.

How to cope? Plan to invest numerous 18-hour days immediately before the visit. Make yourself available. Know the resources of your campus and community and who controls them. Use your people network, and delegate responsibility to those whom you can trust to get the job done. Be prepared to answer every question and to carry out directions quickly and completely. If you are hosting a foreign dignitary, research the customs of his or her country, especially traditional welcoming ceremonies. International faculty members are good resources for assistance. For questions of protocol, telephone the country's embassy in Washington, DC, and ask to speak to the cultural attaché.

The plans of government officials often change at the last minute because of political crises on the domestic or international scene, so it is always wise to have a backup program in case your guest cancels. I once spent a frantic week preparing for a visit to our campus from the Secretary of State. Plans called for him to land by helicopter on the lawn in front of the alumni center, join a group of state and local VIPs for luncheon, and give a public speech that evening before flying back to Washington. All luncheon guests had been checked through security. All guests were required to be seated at their places to await his arrival. Excitement built as we heard the helicopters approaching in the distance and finally landing. Moments later, the secretary trotted into the room, hastily announced he couldn't stay, and walked out as quickly as he had arrived. For a few moments, stunned guests sat with their mouths agape and then rushed to watch the helicopter lift off. Few bothered to return to eat their lunch, and I spent the afternoon canceling arrangements.

Dignitary visits can be very expensive because plans are often made at the last minute, forcing you to pay a premium. Generators may be needed to provide the extra electrical power needed by the media. You may wind up renting props like TV-compatible blue backdrapes, or portable bleachers might be needed to accommodate guests.

Develop, as well as you can, a projected budget estimating the additional expenses associated with the VIP's appearance, and draw up a plan for acquiring the money to cover it. Luckily, many corporate and private donors are eager to have their names associated with the appearance of an important official. To help you plan, call the special events planner at another institution that has previously hosted your guest, or a person of similar rank, and glean every bit of information possible.

One planner who is a veteran of numerous dignitary events says, "Keep things in perspective. You're bombarded with myriad details, and you have to reconcile early on that everything may not be done perfectly due to constraints in time and resources. You need to establish and focus on the real priorities."

• • •

Plan for the Worst

Talk to any group of special events planners and you'll find almost every one of them has an emergency story to tell: The workshop speaker who suddenly fainted, the ballroom that flooded when a pipe burst, the dangerous crush of spectators into a stadium's stairwells when a storm came up.

Do you have an emergency plan for every event and each venue? Be prepared for the worst by making preparations to avoid problems and knowing what to do if an emergency does happen.

Understanding potential risks and taking safeguards for dealing with them is step one of a good emergency plan. While most planners develop contingencies for everything from burned-out projector bulbs to too little food, many forget to consider possibilities like medical emergencies, fire, tornadoes, earthquakes, and bomb threats.

Early in the planning process, meet with campus security and risk managers to assess plans. Include a review of all activities, venues, and insurance coverages. If your event is being held in a hotel or other facility, ask for a briefing on the property's emergency plan from its risk managers and security representatives.

Inspect the site to be certain it is large enough to handle the crowd and its parking needs. Outdoor events must conform to local fire and safety codes, especially if you plan to erect a tent. Violations can mean not only endangering guests but risking stiff fines or the event's being shut down at the last minute.

Inadequate or poorly managed parking might put people in danger of getting hurt in traffic or make your institution liable when cars are parked on private property without permission. Do a walk-through to learn the location of exits, fire extinguishers, stairways, and emergency telephones. Be certain facilities meet local fire and safety codes for the required number of sprinklers, fire extinguishers, and emergency lighting. If you are using a tent or installing decor such as ceiling tenting or fabric draping, require vendors to show proof that their goods are treated to be flame retardant.

Consider how susceptible the location is to seasonal natural disasters such as snowstorms, tornadoes, hurricanes, or floods. Even if it's not severe-weather season, it is wise to set a rain date and publicize it.

Investigate what else is planned for the same day that might cause congestion or affect parking or access to facilities.

Be aware of the increased risk for violent behavior that can be associated with appearances by dignitaries, celebrities, religious leaders, political leaders or candidates, and representatives of various causes. If your event or speakers may be controversial or provoke demonstrations, plan extra measures for crowd control, communication, and bomb threats. Know the protocol for relaying emergency information through layers of security personnel including those on-site as well as local and state authorities.

Review room setups to ensure exits and aisles are not blocked, exit doors are unlocked, and floors are not slippery. Post directional signs and barricades to restrict crowd movement into undesirable areas.

Be sure all walkways, parking lots, and remote areas of the venue are adequately lighted. Have security patrols in all locations.

Plan to complete all construction, such as staging and the installation of bleacher seating, far enough in advance to safety test it before the event.

Write a comprehensive emergency plan and conduct a training session on the procedures for all event workers.

If your event is by reservation, keep a list of guests with you so that a head count can be easily conducted in an evacuation situation.

• • •

Protect Your Guests

For each venue, develop a crowd-control strategy, and determine and enforce a manageable number of guests. Too many people can overwhelm vendors, suppliers, and facilities and lead to bad behavior and injuries.

Plan evacuation procedures and prepare for medical emergencies. All large events should include first-aid stations staffed with certified emergency medical personnel. Post signs telling the station's location. Include emergency information in event brochures and announce procedures at the beginning of the meeting or event.

• • •

Protect Yourself

Planners today are at risk for liability lawsuits stemming from the events they plan. You can be held liable for financial losses resulting from everything from entertainers who don't perform as advertised to claims resulting from property damage and personal injury. It is incorrect to assume that you are protected by school-sponsored or -purchased insurance. You're probably not. Here are some ways to diminish the chances of being sued.

Know your insurance situation and the laws of your state. Start by asking your campus risk management or insurance officer, legal counsel, or the vice president for administration.

Require vendors, suppliers, musicians, and people who rent or use your facility to have adequate liability insurance that also extends protection to your institution. Request a copy of the policy.

Always have a contract. Get all agreements in writing, and be certain contracts contain language that protects and indemnifies you and your university. Hotel contracts for use of facilities protect them. Provide an addendum to the contract that also protects you. Avoid signing contracts yourself. Instead, have the highest officer possible (someone at the vice president's level or above) sign all contracts, especially for events where alcohol will be served.

Prepare for the worst by writing an emergency plan and training all staff members in procedures for medical emergencies, building evacuations, fire, and other catastrophes. Hold regular training sessions, and write a protocol for handling emergencies. List who is in charge in case of emergency and procedures to be followed. In the event of a lawsuit, you may be asked to produce a copy of this document and proof of staff training. Having and following such a plan can reduce your vulnerability.

In addition to a general liability policy, you may want to consider coverages for event cancellation or prize payouts.

Cancellation insurance protects your institution from the substantial expenses that can occur in case an event has to be canceled or postponed such as if a performer becomes ill or a facility under construction isn't ready as planned.

Prize-indemnity insurance protects you when you are running a promotion that involves an unusually large prize, such as a hole-in-one contest. If someone wins, the cost of the prize is covered.

• • •

Social Host Liability

When alcohol has been served, planners may be held liable as social hosts for accidents involving their guests, both when they are on campus and when they are on the road. The best protection is simply not to serve alcohol at any university events.

Barring that, have alcohol served only by trained professionals who are adequately covered by a social host or other insurance policy. Many of the large corporations that supply food service on college campuses have such insurance. When they cater your events and supply bartenders, you may be protected under their social host policy. Check first, ask questions, and don't take anyone's word for it—read the policy yourself.

Moving an event to a hotel or conference facility does not automatically transfer liability to them. Before sponsoring events at hotels, conference centers, and the like, investigate their social host and other insurance coverages.

Many hotels don't carry alcohol policies at all or carry coverage only for their own employees or their own sponsored events. Your institution or organization must be named as an "additional insured" party in order to be covered on such as policy.

Ask to see a copy of the hotel or facility policy. Read the exclusions, and call the company listed on the declaration sheet to be sure. You will likely find that private parties are not covered.

• • •

Style: Some Have It, Some Don't

Style is that elusive quality that makes special events stand out. It is the intangible ingredient in this complex planning mix that makes the difference between flat and fantastic, between an event people will remember and talk about long after it is over and one they will have forgotten by the next evening. One planner says style is conspicuous by not seeming to be there at all.

Style comes from devoting the same care to the tiniest detail behind the scenes that you use to select a speaker or a hall. It is a blend of creativity and imagination that, when well cultivated, becomes your signature on every event you stage.

Develop you own style by studying what other special events planners do and attending other organizations' functions. Read books about entertaining and lifestyle and keep up with trends in foods, wines, music, and decorating. Incorporate these trends into the traditions of your school, college, or university and don't be afraid to try new approaches to "old" events.

People love presents, and a well-planned special event is a kind of present. You want your guests to have all the pleasure of opening a pretty package to find a wonderful surprise. With practice, you can begin to develop a sense of what elements constitute a well-planned, well-organized affair that is tastefully and graciously executed. You can begin to recognize those components that make up style.

It doesn't matter if you're planning a reunion luncheon for the 14th year in a row or a completely new black-tie gala to launch a major capital campaign. Your guests will notice and appreciate the time you took to make the event extra special.

• • •

Making It Work

You don't need a degree in hotel and restaurant management to make arrangements for special events, but it does help if you develop a working knowledge of the terminology and standard procedures.

Whether you are planning an event in your university union or at a posh resort hotel, the planning details and the sequence of decisions are essentially the same:

1. Be certain that the purpose of your function has been clearly defined.
2. Identify the goals and objectives of the event.
3. Develop a fairly accurate idea of the number of people planning to attend.
4. Select an appropriate facility that is compatible with your budget.
5. Construct an outline of all the elements to incorporate, from promotion and registration to audiovisuals and insurance.
6. Determine the theme, color, and decoration scheme.
7. Decide on food, beverages, and entertainment.
8. Prepare an order of events, timed to the minute.
9. Plan the billing process and follow-up procedures.

Now, think small. Concentrate on the details of everything. Good special events planners are perfectionists with a flair for presentation, precision, and minutiae.

Picture yourself taking part in this event from the moment you receive the invitation: Imagine how you will respond, how you will travel to the event, where you will park, the route you will walk, what you will see upon entering, who will greet you, what you will do next, what you will eat, what it will be served on, what you will drink and what you will drink from, how the program will be introduced, what the lighting will look like, how the event will be concluded, and how you will depart.

Success hinges on attention to detail. And coordinating the hundreds of details involved in a special event is an enormous task.

Different people have different methods for keeping details straight. Among these are check-off sheets, notebooks, and daily files. Computer software is available to help you manage everything from the guest list to room setups. As you gain experience, you will no doubt develop a system particularly suited to your work style. I use a daily file system where I file notes for everything that must be accomplished according to date. One secret I have learned to prevent a last-minute crunch is to complete each task in the daily file so that nothing is deferred or forgotten.

But the number-one secret to success is good communication. It is impossible to pull off a successful event by yourself. Good, solid planning involves hours of behind-the-scenes brainstorming, meetings, explaining, selling, and coordinating to make certain everything and everybody winds-up in exactly the right place at exactly the right time.

To help accomplish this, delegate as many details as possible to the experts in each area and keep a stream of communication going between yourself and the committee, the caterer, the florist, the entertainers, the printer, campus VIPs, maintenance staff, the equipment rental firm, security personnel, and anyone else who has a role in the event. All must be kept up-to-date and constantly reminded of their responsibilities. Good communication increases the commitment of all concerned by emphasizing their importance to the success of the event and giving everyone a feeling of ownership.

CHAPTER 2

Spread the Word: Invitations, Tickets, and Publicity

WHEN AN INVITATION ARRIVES IN THE mail, it must compete with the daily deluge of junk mail, bills, and catalogs crammed into the mailbox. Your invitation must stand out in that fistful of mail and say "open me" and "read me." Yet at the same time, it must be consistent with your event and your institution's image.

The invitation creates the first impression most people will have of your special event. Often it provides the only information they will have on which to decide whether or not to attend. The way your invitation looks—"sophisticated," "important," "fun," or "boring"—often does more to convey the tone and character of your event than do the words. Help make that decision a positive one by using your invitation to create excitement about your event and to answer any questions your potential guest may have.

Work with a graphic designer to create the look you want and then incorporate it into the invitation and all other printed materials associated with the event such as programs, menu cards, posters, and even decorations. One event planner refers to this paper trail as the "footprint" of the event, noting that often printed materials are all that is left behind to tell your story. One prestigious university with ties to our nation's Founding Fathers commissioned an artist to make engravings of campus landmarks with the same look as the renderings used on United States currency. The images were pressed onto handmade paper. The result communicated sophistication, tradition, and affluence to alumni invited to the school's black-tie capital campaign kickoff event. Not only was the event a success, the invitations and matching programs have become collector's items.

The best way to get your invitation opened is to make it look like that increasingly rare item, a personal letter. This means using high-quality stationery and hand addressing envelopes. Never use computer labels. Your recipient knows that computers spit out junk mail; people address envelopes. Most junk mail is never opened. Virtually all handwritten mail is opened and read.

Use a stamp, preferably an attractive commemorative, and never use a postage meter. You want to make your envelope look as much like a personal letter as possible. Junk mail and bills come with a bulk rate or meter mark. Some business mail comes with generic stamps. A commemorative stamp helps your invitation attract attention and you may even find a design that depicts your theme.

The invitation itself should include who, what, when, where, and how much. Be specific about the site of your function, particularly if it is at a hotel chain that has more than one property in your city. If guests from out of town will attend, include a map and phone number for help in identifying your location.

Give consideration to creative invitations as a way to capture the attention of VIPs and to generate publicity for your event. One university was seeking money to support its collection of French art. The event planners chose a Parisian-cafe theme and surprised prospective guests by having a "French" waiter deliver each invitation tucked into a basket of freshly baked croissants. Another university sent singing messengers to each guest's doorstep with the invitation to a musical event. Invitations to an event introducing a new basketball coach consisted of boxed, miniature basketballs nestled in recyclable packing chips in team colors. Such creativity costs time and money but often pays great dividends if you can match an appropriate promotion to your event.

Savvy planners ask committee members to write personal notes on invitations to encourage their friends and associates to attend. Simple lines such as "Mary and Fred, we hope you will join us. This promises to be great fun," signed by a committee member, can go a long way toward bolstering responses. The same committee members can follow up outstanding invitations with telephone calls a few weeks later. One caution: Use personal notes only on first-class mail; personal notes are not permitted in bulk mail.

A response mechanism is an integral part of every invitation. Sometimes it is simply a phone number for call-in responses. Most of the time it will be a reply card and a self-addressed envelope. If you are asking for payment with the reply card, make sure that the envelope is large enough to hold both the card and a check.

When your event is a fund-raiser, include a line on the RSVP card to encourage guests who cannot attend to send a contribution. An event I planned recently netted $14,000 because the reply card included a line that said, "I/we cannot attend. A contribution for $_____ is enclosed."

For guests who are purchasing an entire table, provide printed lines on the back of the reply card so they can write the names of the people they have invited to sit at their table.

When planning a formal event and invitation, consult an etiquette book for proper wording, format, and correct forms of address.

Check postal regulations for size and weight restrictions to make sure that your invitation meets standards and will require no extra postage. The postal service can reject your invitation for being too small, too large, or too flimsy or for lacking a return address. Never write personal messages inside bulk mail or insert pages in some pieces but not others. Doing so might disqualify your mailing for bulk rate because this class of mail requires each piece to be identical. The U.S. Postal Service offers booklets explaining size, weight, and addressing requirements for each class of mail. Copies are available at the post office window.

• • •

Organize Your Mailing List

Whether you are issuing 500 or 10,000 invitations, a database that will get the job done accurately and efficiently is imperative. Solve this problem by creating a useful database that tells each person's affiliation in terms of volunteer involvement, board status, donor record, and other helpful clues. Here's another solid reason for investing the time to create such a file: It helps prevent the erosion of institutional history caused by the passing of time and staff turnover. Make space in your database to note, for instance, that the person is a former board member, is the fourth generation of a family to graduate from your institution, or is the granddaughter of the person for whom the administration building is named. Store important personal notes that may save you from disaster. Once when I was new at a job, I gave my first event seating chart to my new boss for perusal. She immediately noticed a serious error. Not being familiar with the constituents, I had seated a single woman, who happened to be the city's mayor, and a couple at the same table thinking they were relatives because they had the same last name. In fact, the trio consisted of the mayor, her ex-husband, and his new wife, and they weren't on speaking terms!

Begin your events database by learning about your institution's database program for tracking alumni and donors. Chances are the tools are already in place via a system used to track donor records. Most modern fund-raising software can easily handle this function. Using it may be simply a matter of getting the special events office connected and equipping staff with the know-how to run the program.

Keeping guest lists updated with correct titles, addresses, phone numbers, and spouses' names can save time and trouble. Never let old information sit in a file to be corrected later; it is too easy to forget to do it, and, inevitably, you will embarrass yourself by mailing an invitation to an old address or by including the name of an ex-spouse.

Your data file can include information on invitations extended and accepted. Plus, by tracking invitations you can prevent inviting the same people time and again to the same kinds of functions or inviting them to back-to-back events. On days when several offices may be inviting guests, using a database will prevent issuing duplicate invitations.

One caveat: Resist the temptation to develop your own invitation database at your desktop. Inevitably you will become a disconnected island of outdated information. Instead, engage the cooperation of other campus offices to keep one, central database up to date and coded so that it can be easily sorted. Such a database will enable you to pull an accurate list quickly to meet your needs.

You will need access to the following information:

- both spouses' complete names;

- both spouses' business or professional affiliations;
- home address;
- home phone;
- business addresses;
- business phones;
- e-mail addresses;
- donor level;
- connection with the institution (graduation class years, colleges, and/or the same information for their children);
- special interests such as music, art, theater, athletics, or an academic area;
- important personal information, such as food preferences or need for a handicapped parking permit; and
- record of invitations extended and accepted.

• • •

Inviting Thousands?

Are you prepared to handle the logistics of issuing personal invitations to a large number of people, say 5,000? Milestone events such as anniversary celebrations, building dedications, and presidential inaugurations typically involve inviting thousands of your institution's closest friends. Among a group of colleges and universities that recently hosted inaugurations, the smallest number of invitations sent was 1,000; the largest was 17,000. One planner had one month to organize and issue invitations for 10,500. All agreed that formulating a guest list and managing the invitation process was the most time-consuming, troublesome aspect of the entire celebration.

Because major occasions draw guests from across the spectrum of constituents, each function demands a customized list to ensure that the appropriate people are included. As celebration plans develop, the complexity of the invitation process is frequently overlooked—until it becomes a problem.

One planner told a nightmarish story of multiple sets of invitations being mixed up and sent to the wrong people and an entire order of custom-made envelopes being ruined with incorrect addresses.

Another planner, whose invitation list wound up consisting of 7,541 names, said her university assembled a "management information team" that "spent a whole lot of time" planning the invitation process, including designing a special computer program.

Whether you are issuing 500 or 10,000 invitations, a system that will get the job done accurately and efficiently is imperative. Having an accurate list and developing a realistic work plan are the two keys to success.

Here are some suggestions that work:

- Start early. Nine months or more before the event is the time to start developing a guest list.
- Put one person in charge. Designate an invitations chair responsible for

assembling and managing the guest list; establishing deadlines; and supervising the addressing, stuffing and mailing process. Choose someone who knows your constituents, understands computers, and has experience with mailing lists.

- Set a deadline. Establish a cutoff date for submitting names.
- Make a master list. To avoid overlooking anyone, ask for lists of VIPs from the deans, vice presidents, athletics, development, alumni, the president's office, and anyone else who will play a role in the celebration. Typically, such lists will be from personal computer files in formats that are not compatible with yours and will be out of date, missing key pieces of information (such as first names), and not in alphabetical or zip-code order. The easiest way to organize and sort these raw lists is to make a master list by loading all the information into a computer. This eliminates the tedious practice of cross-referencing paper lists or alphabetizing by hand. The new master list also will be handy later to track reservations or generate labels for follow-up mailings.
- Get expert advice. Discuss your needs with campus computer experts before you begin so that data get entered in a way that enables you to retrieve useful information. You will need the capability to sort and merge the list.
- Code everyone. Because large events typically include several versions of invitations as well as inserts for private functions, developing a computer coding system to track people by group is imperative. For example: If you are planning an inauguration, a general invitation would be used for alumni and friends. The university trustees would receive special invitations to the ceremony, a brunch preceding it, and a reception following. Their invitations might also include information on special parking and a response card for ordering academic regalia. Faculty would receive an invitation that is worded differently from one sent to visiting delegates of other schools.
- Brainstorm database categories with the planning committee. Trustees, major donors, faculty, emeriti faculty, elected officials, administrators, alumni and foundation board members, and platform participants are just a few. Many people will fall into several categories. A newspaper publisher may appear on three raw lists: VIP members of the media, alumni, and major donors. The ability to sort and merge the list can spare you the embarrassment of sending the same person several invitations.
- Check and double-check. Once the list is computerized, divide it into pages, and have a team of staffers and key volunteers review it. The team can pare the list down, proofread it for misspellings, catch duplicates, and make sure all information is complete. Watch for slight variations of the same names that result in two listings. Identify names that require double-checking: Some examples are deceased, divorced, or remarried persons and those who are listed by a business instead of home address.

- Make corrections. Assign someone to research missing information and load all corrections into the computer. Print out a report of the number of invitations needed in each category.
- Order the invitations according to the number of people in each group. (If you are using bulk mail, remember to imprint the envelopes with your permit.)
- Print out at least one copy of your entire list in alphabetical order for reference. It should display the codes assigned to each name so you can quickly determine to which group a person belongs.
- First class or bulk? Whether or not you are using first-class mail will determine the order in which names are given to volunteers for addressing. If you are using first class, print the lists in alphabetical order. If you are using bulk mail, print them in zip-code order.
- Divide and conquer. Computer-generate lists according to the groups you have chosen. To help you keep track of which list is being used, color-code each printout by marking it with a highlighter. Number the pages.
- Double-check! Spot check to be sure that names selected on VIP lists do not still appear on the general list.
- Secure the lists. To avoid mix-ups, one person should be in charge of the printouts and have all copies. Don't let several copies get into circulation because of the danger of accidentally double-sending sections of any one list.
- Hand or computer lettering? If envelopes will be hand-addressed, recruit a team of volunteers. Keep in mind that one person writing at a steady pace can complete about 50 invitations in an hour.
- Computer-generated script or calligraphy is acceptable, provided printing can be done directly on the envelopes, not on labels.
- Organize an addressing party in a large, well-lit room equipped with tables and chairs where materials can be left out until the job is done.
- Visit the post office. For first class mail, select and purchase a beautiful stamp or one in keeping with your theme. Self-adhesive stamps will speed the process but are available in a limited choice of designs.
- If you are using bulk mail, check the latest requirements for sorting and bundling, be certain your permit has been paid, and find out if payment for postage is required in advance.
- Plan a production line. Divide workers by task, and set up stations for addressing, stuffing, stamping, and sealing. Assign one or two people to collect finished components and move them to the next station.
- Provide supplies. You'll need plenty of fresh black pens (preferably roller-ball or fine-point felt tips), stick-on notes, return-address rubber stamps and ink pads (if using), and squeeze-bottle moisteners and a pitcher of water for refilling. Also handy: scratch pads, rubber bands, paper clips, highlighter markers, scissors, and boxes.

- Train workers. Explain the process and how to properly address an envelope. Make posters to illustrate formats. Be specific on inevitable questions, such how to address to single people (Ms. Mary Jones and Guest or simply Ms. Mary Jones). Prepare a sample of the completed invitation and a list of what goes in each envelope. Ask people to mark questionable addresses on the printouts with a highlighter so these can be corrected later.
- Ready, set, address! Assign each volunteer a section of the list. As sections are completed, collect and file them. (If a volunteer must leave before completing her list, have it returned to you instead of being passed on to someone else. This will help prevent envelopes from getting out of order.)
- Keep the envelopes in order. Completed envelopes must be kept in the same order in which the names appeared on the list. Use the boxes the envelopes were delivered in, and put one at each addresser's place. Mark each box with the list and page numbers it contains to make it easier to retrieve or insert an envelope should the need arise. Numbered boxes will also prevent a bulk mailing from getting out of order. Be sure everyone knows the importance of keeping envelopes in order throughout the entire preparation process. At one work session, two volunteers performed the final step—sealing the envelopes. Unknowingly, they undid hours of careful work because they tossed the invitations randomly into a big box instead of keeping them in zip-code order.

More tips:

- To avoid mix-ups, work with only one type of invitation at a time.
- Address the envelopes before stuffing or stamping. Empty envelopes are easier to write on, and if there's a mistake, a stamp isn't wasted.
- Don't let workers take invitations home to address, mail, or deliver in person. It is too easy to procrastinate or forget. One volunteer asked her husband to drop 100 invitations in the mail on his way to work; she found them in his car glove box several months after the event.
- Provide refreshments. Serve beverages and non-sticky snacks in an area away from printed materials.

• • •

When to Mail Invitations

For a major event, consider sending a "save the date" card as soon as you have targeted a date. In some instances, that could be as many as six to eight months or even a year in advance. This card says that your organization is planning to have a function on a certain date, mentions the name and nature of the event, and asks the person to reserve the date on the calendar. State that a formal invitation will follow.

The timing of the mailing of invitations should depend on your audience, the nature of the event, whether you're inviting only local people, and your own planning requirements. Four weeks ahead may be fine for a local group; if you mail too early, people will set your invitation aside while they wait to see what other obligations or invitations come up. But four weeks may be insufficient for out-of-town guests. Although you should stick to the etiquette book for invitations to very formal affairs, the timing of other invitations to generate maximum attendance takes both experimentation and guesswork.

For some events, such as an ongoing luncheon lecture series or a late-afternoon cocktail party to meet a new coach, less than three weeks' notice may result in more participation. At one medical college, invitations issued one week before a monthly luncheon for doctors generated an excellent response; those invitations that had been mailed earlier were ignored. Etiquette expert Letitia Baldrige suggests three weeks before a cocktail or tea party; four to six weeks before a breakfast, lunch, dinner party, or evening reception; six months before a major all-day or two-day meeting.

• • •

Repondez s'il vous plait

RSVP means "please reply," but many people do not, especially if they are not planning to attend. Assuming that no response equals a "no" can be a risky business, however, even though it often seems to hold true. If you are within a few days of an event and have many responses outstanding, one option is to call those people and inquire about their intentions.

Another way to collect responses is to put "regrets only" and a phone number in the lower left-hand corner of the invitation. People are supposed to call if they are not coming and if you don't hear from them, you can presume they're coming. Of course, many people will ignore this request as well, and your counts for food and beverages can be way off.

If you experience great difficulty in getting responses, don't feel alone. Even noted etiquette expert Letitia Baldrige reports a growing "RSVP problem." Many, many people—of all social stations—simply do not respond to invitations, whether they plan to show up or not.

An even more serious problem for event planners is the no-show—people who accept an invitation and then change their minds without bothering to inform you. At a recent dinner event, 74 of the 325 guests who returned RSVP cards saying they would attend were no-shows. The total cost for these ill-mannered people was $1,480. Some institutions and charities now bill no-shows for the costs of food and other items reserved for them.

When an accurate count is absolutely critical, some special events planners resort to telephoning guests two or three days ahead to confirm their plans. Others figure at least a 10-percent no-show rate and reduce guaranteed reservation counts accordingly. Under no circumstances should you give in to a last-minute case of nerves and raise guarantees on the concern that more people will show up than the number for which you planned. Veteran planners agree that the number of unexpected guests who walk in is very low. If there are any, they will virtually always be offset by no-shows.

Offering the convenience of high-tech ways to reply may improve the RSVP rate, especially when events are targeted to younger audiences who are comfortable using e-mail, telephone voice mail, and faxes for everyday communication. Technology's immediacy can move potential guests from thinking about your event to actually replying. While you may not be comfortable promoting e-mail replies to your most formal invitations, for many events such as workshops, reunions, and symposia, it is appropriate and welcome. Computer correspondence via e-mail also makes it easier to clear up questions rather than by playing phone tag.

In addition to e-mail and fax, offer a 24-hour-a-day dedicated events telephone line to take reservations. Record an outgoing greeting giving callers directions for leaving replies or requesting additional information. Make the outgoing message succinct and easy to understand, and don't require callers to keep pressing buttons. Set the telephone to answer on the first or second ring.

Facilitate your fast-response system by printing e-mail, fax, and phone numbers prominently on program announcements, advertisements, and fliers.

If you are selling tickets or charging for an event, make it clear that reservations are not confirmed until they are paid in full. Requiring people to pay in advance will greatly reduce the number of no-shows, and if people don't show up, you still have the money to cover costs. Collecting money beforehand also prevents the necessity of handling cash and processing credit cards at the door. State a policy that no refunds will be issued after a certain date.

The best way to facilitate advance payments is to ask people to pay by check or credit card. Offering a "bill me" option will also work, but you may still find yourself on the day of the event with unpaid reservations. Another disadvantage of billing people is that the process generates lots of work for office staff, and collection can sometimes drag out for months. Before agreeing to bill people, it's wise to remember an old event planners axiom: It's hard to get people to pay for food they've already eaten and fun they've already enjoyed.

• • •

Tickets

Tickets are probably the most efficient, least expensive method of controlling costs, guaranteeing revenue, and sorting out the cast of characters.

If you have contracted to use a facility such as a theater, an auditorium, or the stadium on your own campus, these types of facilities usually have a full-time ticket office and staff. Managing tickets for a large event, such as a concert or a celebrity appearance, is a monumental job. Don't assume that your staff has the time or expertise to do it. Negotiate with the ticket people of the facility to have them manage tickets for you. In fact, many large facilities require that you use their staff as part of the rental agreement. This protects them and also frees you and your staff to concentrate on other things.

For small-scale events, such as banquets and on-campus lectures, tickets serve as income guarantees and help provide security so that only paying guests gain access. For these kinds of events, you can probably manage tickets on your own with the help of diligent staff members and a personal computer. Software is available to perform these tasks.

Tickets should be mailed the same day that each order or affirmative RSVP arrives. When people accept too close to the date of the event to receive tickets by mail, call them and explain that their tickets will be held at a "will call" window at the door. Remind them of forms of payment that will be accepted.

Whether the event is paid or free, you should keep an accurate record of all responses to invitations, both positive and negative. Record the date tickets are mailed as well as all money received. An alphabetical list of guests who have been mailed tickets and others who have clearance to enter should be available at the door. This allows staff to check tickets as people arrive and prevent crashers from entering. Instruct your staff on the procedure to follow if a person insists upon admission but is not on the list.

Decide beforehand whether or not you will mail tickets to those who sent no payment or inadequate payment with their RSVP. Set a firm policy about ticket sales at the door. Handling ticket money at the door requires additional staff to keep traffic flowing. You'll also need supplies such as tickets, change, a credit card reader (which means a phone line) or an imprinter, a telephone for check or charge verification (if required by your bank), a cash box, and receipts. If you plan to connect a computer, you will need a power source and possibly a phone jack.

• • •

Pricing

When you are pricing tickets, take all expenses into account, tally them, add a 15-percent contingency fee, and divide by the total capacity of the facility. This will give you the per-person cost of the event. Multiply by two. This is the minimum price you can charge per ticket and expect to break even—that is, if you're lucky and unanticipated expenses don't run high. When calculating expenses, always remember to include less obvious expenses, such as complimentary tickets for VIPs, overtime pay for security, and cost overruns due to missed deadlines and last-minute extras.

Remember that for this formula to keep you out of red ink, you need to sell all available tickets. Many a special events planner has been in hot water because ticket sales did not meet projections, yet expenses still had to be covered. You should consider the consequences of this possibility before you commit to an event. If breaking even or losing money will ruin your special events budget for the entire year, or if you have no resources to cover deficits, either scrap the event or find a cosponsor to share or offset some of the costs.

• • •

Tickets for Fund-raising Events

Tickets for fund-raising events rarely come in one denomination but are often priced at several levels, each featuring various perquisites and recognitions designed to induce people to pay a premium. You can create ticket levels for any event, whether it is a sporting event, a gallery opening, a celebrity concert, a world premiere of a movie, or a gala dinner and dance. Ticket leveling helps ensure budget stability and adds an air of prestige that appeals to many donors and thus increases income.

How many ticket levels you will offer, how much they will cost, and what perks you will include depend on what makes sense for your project. Consider the affluence of your potential audience and the nature of your event. The more exclusive the event, the more you can charge.

How many levels?

Offering three levels of ticket prices is usually manageable, but having many more becomes unwieldy. The base or "general admission" ticket should be just that—it is the lowest in price and it covers expenses and includes at least a 50-percent markup as a donation. If the event costs are very low and it won't price you out of the market, push this markup to 65 percent. Generally speaking, half of all ticket sales will come from this level.

Next, offer a mid-level ticket. This covers expenses and represents a larger donation. In return, the purchaser receives perks such as better seats, preferred parking, and mention in the program.

Finally, offer a high-priced "patron-level" ticket. Sales from this level will represent a small number of your greatest supporters, led by the event chair (you hope) and persons who are already major donors to the area that will be benefited. Corporations may also contribute at this level. All patron-level donors receive VIP treatment and extra perks as well as plenty of public recognition. Patron tickets should include a significant donation.

Perks make it work

Perks can include things like printing patrons' names in the program or offering them reserved parking or preferred seating. At the highest ticket levels, perks should include all of the things given to lower-level patrons, plus goodies like a backstage party to meet the entertainers, a private reception with dignitaries, or an autographed copy of a visiting author's book, as well as public recognition in all event-related printed materials. When adding perks to higher ticket levels, choose those that increase your costs only slightly or not at all.

How much is deductible?

Certainly tax benefits can play a significant role in event ticket sales—particularly patron level tickets.

Tax laws will continue to change so it is important that you regularly check with your institution's gift-receiving professionals and tax advisors. Their interpretations may affect your ticket strategy, invitation wording, and attendee receipts and acknowledgments.

Here are some basics event planners should know:

- The Internal Revenue Service does not consider tickets to be fully deductible because the purchaser does receive some value by attending the event.
- In general, only the amount paid over the "fair market value" is tax deductible. This amount is not necessarily the same as your cost. So, if you sponsor a golf outing at which guests receive lunch, an afternoon of golf, and take home a sleeve of golf balls and a windbreaker, you must be able to determine the fair market value of this package. If the value is $100 and the guests each pay $1,000, the deductible amount is $900. If the guest buys a ticket and does not attend, the deduction may be $1,000.
- Tax laws require charities to notify donors of the fair market value of events.
- Make sure you understand how these amounts are to be calculated and what donor notification process is required.
- Printing deduction information on your invitations does not substitute for sending receipts. Charities can receive hefty fines for failing to issue receipts.

Complimentary tickets for control and PR

Tickets can also be used very effectively as a public relations tool and as a discreet means for staff to identify VIPs in a crowd. At the annual Memorial Golf Tournament at Muirfield Village Golf Club in Dublin, Ohio, one of the most coveted tickets is not a tournament admission ticket but a ticket to the private villa of tournament host Jack Nicklaus. VIPs from around the country are mailed the prestigious tickets that admit them to the exclusive villa for red-carpet treatment including gourmet hors d'oeuvres, drinks, and the chance to rub elbows with celebrities and other special guests—not to mention the status of being seen entering the place.

You can employ the same concept on your campus by mailing VIP tickets or passes good for admission to special hospitality rooms, to a reception hosted by the president, to a backstage cast party after a theater performance, or to an autograph session with a visiting author. This is a particularly effective and helpful technique when staffers don't know guests. Write the guest's name on the back of the ticket before mailing it. At the event you can quickly check ticket backs to see which invited guests are present. Use this information during the event to be sure important people are appropriately greeted and use the list afterward as a record of contact with your VIPs.

Always make it clear these VIP tickets are "nontransferable" so they cannot be passed along to others. My husband and I once served as the host couple in a private indoor box at the university football stadium. Our guests that day were to have been a very wealthy, socially prominent couple from out-of-town. When they accepted their invitation, their passes and necessary admission credentials were mailed—but not marked nontransferable. On the day of the game, kickoff came and went, but our guests had not arrived. Halfway through the first quarter, instead of Mr. and Mrs. Prominent Donor, two teenage boys dressed in scruffy jeans appeared. To our dismay, we discovered that Mr. and Mrs. Donor had passed the tickets along to friends, who had passed them on to friends, who had passed them on to a third friend who gave them to his son.

• • •

Programs

Printing a program to serve as a memento or as an additional way to raise funds is popular. Programs should include the order of the event; brief biographies of special guests or featured speakers; a listing of all donors, sponsors, and volunteers; and, when appropriate, a description of the event's purpose.

If your event is a banquet, leave a program at each place setting to be certain everyone receives a copy. If you have assigned seating and thus know who is seated where, it is perfectly acceptable and less expensive to leave one program per couple.

• • •

Publicity

Publicity helps accomplish the event's public relations goal of building awareness of your institution and its people and programs. Publicity also serves as a way to publicly recognize honored guests and volunteers. When yours is a fund-raising event, publicity helps sell tickets. The more favorable publicity there is about your event, the more desirable it becomes to attend. Ticket sales benefit as people jump on the bandwagon, and the bandwagon gets rolling through good publicity. It is important, however, to realize that mounting a publicity campaign is not appropriate for every event. It's hard for many special events planners to accept the fact that from an editor's point of view, most events are not newsworthy. The days of newspapers publishing photos of check presentations and devoting space to descriptions of decorations are gone. As a rule of thumb, if the event is by invitation only, it is not a candidate for a publicity campaign.

There are exceptions. If the guest of honor is a Nobel Prize winner, the media may be interested in interviewing her but will probably not be interested in reporting on the black-tie dinner you held in her honor. It is when events are open to the public, especially when they are free, that you will find interest among editors. Examples would be a community open house, a college night for area high school students and their parents, a free performance by a renowned symphony, or a football season "meet the team" scrimmage and picnic.

Working with the PR office

As college or university event planners, the majority of us have the luxury of a professional public relations staff on campus. Whether this office is called "media relations," "news service," "communications," or "public affairs," it is the only office authorized to deal with the media on the institution's behalf.

The staff includes public relations professionals who are trained in journalism, know the formats for the different types of media, and have established relationships with reporters. They know what kinds of stories will interest the media in your area, what reporters will and won't use, and how to time news for best coverage.

Although the existence of the public relations staff means that event planners do not have to shoulder the responsibility of working with the media and promoting events alone—a task that is a full-time job in itself—event planners must be involved in the publicity planning and understand how the media relations function operates. They need to know the basic rules of the publicity game so that their requests will be reasonable and their expectations appropriate.

Here are some tips to help you deal with your PR office:

- Never contact the media yourself. The campus needs to speak with one voice so that messages are clear and news releases and advisories are professionally written and prepared in the correct format. This is the exclusive domain of the PR office.
- Involve the public relations staff very early in the planning process. This will allow the opportunity to make suggestions that can maximize publicity. Early involvement provides the chance to identify and release many stories to keep awareness of the event high. Magazines, like the alumni publication or regional publications that can be a very effective source of publicity, often have deadlines four to six months in advance. A well-planned publicity campaign includes coverages timed to support important points on the road to success—the beginning of the public ticket sales, for example, or the announcement of a big-name entertainer as your headliner.
- PR professionals know how to pitch a story and find a news angle that will prove irresistible. Events attract the most media attention after the fact. That won't help you sell tickets, but it will help accomplish PR goals and build attendance in subsequent years.
- Determine who will be interested in the news, what aspects of the news will be useful to them, and how to reach these people.
- Plan publicity to further your objectives; then direct information to the most appropriate outlets, whether print, radio, or television.
- Tailor the message to media deadlines and style.
- Plan publicity in proportion to the need. A few well-placed phone calls and personal visits may be sufficient to bolster attendance at a banquet, whereas a full-scale publicity campaign may be needed to create excitement for a major art exhibition.
- Schedule publicity to attain repeated mentions. Don't rely on one news release to make a single big splash for you. Announce the main speaker;

then announce honored guests; then, immediately before the big day, follow up with details of the program.

When you are sponsoring a program that lasts for several days or a week, such as a conference on genetics research or a symposium on the arts, you should report on proceedings with daily news releases.

If you have a corporate sponsor, the public relations staff also takes charge of coordinating your school's press relations efforts with those of the corporate PR office. Coordinating with the corporate PR office means joint releases can be made, thus helping to ensure coverage, and that confidential information is not released.

• • •

Formal Approaches to Publicity

The public relations staff builds a media plan around the event based on the important happenings in the planning timeline. For example, during a year-long anniversary observance, staffers may begin by researching interesting historical facts, finding archival photos, and identifying people to interview. With angles and interviews determined, the PR staff determines the appropriate media outlets and packages the news accordingly. The staff may choose news releases, exclusive interviews, photo sessions, tours, video news releases for television, "actualities" for radio (comments given by telephone), or a news conference to get the word out. Skilled practitioners can identify specialized outlets for stories that may not be obvious at first. Perhaps the new computer technology that will be used during the entertainment portion of your event would be of interest to the local science writer, or the food and wine editor may run a story about the award-winning regional wines that will be served at the dinner.

A good media plan contains a mixture of several techniques and outlets, each aimed at the target audience through the medium it uses most. Sending news releases to the local daily paper with a 350,000 circulation may do nothing for your event, while an article in the alumni magazine will generate a flood of ticket sales.

Concentrate on local coverage

Most publicity will be centered on the local media because they reach the people who are most interested in happenings on campus and most likely to attend or to be involved in a volunteer capacity. It is difficult to get national coverage unless the event speaker is a prominent political figure such as the President of the United States or the head of a foreign country.

Look for the local angle in news stories. A news release describing your gala may hit the trash, but when it also announces that the biggest corporation in town is donating $100,000 to sponsor the event, the story becomes newsworthy. If you want local coverage, rather than saying that an event will be held to help construct a new building on campus, focus on how the building will benefit the community.

Local society editors are an important outlet for events news. They are usually interested in prominent committee members and will sometimes attend the event.

Remember to send them invitations, and be prepared to help them find important people in the crowd for interviews, comments, or photos. Cultivate society writers and editors, and read their columns faithfully to learn what and whom they cover. To encourage coverage, offer society writers exclusive information or an interview with the event's honored guest. If society writers attend the event, seat them with interesting and important people, but not at the same table with writers from competing newspapers.

The chances for local television coverage increase dramatically when on-air personalities participate in event planning or take part in event activities that are offbeat and highly visual. A Houston charity recently garnered excellent television coverage by inviting local TV personalities to drive go-carts in a fund-raising race. All three major local stations carried the event during their evening newscasts.

If you are sponsoring a large event that is open to the public, inviting a local radio station to broadcast live from the event site is powerful publicity for you, and it is good advertising for the station.

Don't overlook offering volunteers, special guests, or committee members to appear on locally produced television or radio talk shows. Hosts of such programs are always interested in fresh ideas and usually have air time to fill.

Campus media

Student newspapers, faculty and staff periodicals, Internet listservs, intranet services, World Wide Web sites, and campus radio and television stations are important outlets. Develop on-campus interest in a major special event through a series of stories in the campus press. Maintain a constant flow of news, including coverage of your committee's progress and exclusive interviews with event leaders.

Always treat campus media as equals to external media. Invite representatives to all press conferences and briefings, and put them on the mailing list for news releases. Don't be surprised if campus reporting is not always favorable, but resist the temptation to complain to the editor or faculty advisor about negative stories.

• • •

Informal Approaches to Publicity

With the professional media in the capable hands of the public relations staff, you can turn your attention to informal publicity channels. A successful fund raiser says his best technique for promoting events is having friends ask friends to get involved. This is where the strength of your volunteer leadership and the enthusiasm of committee members prove invaluable.

One of the event's standing committees should be public relations or publicity. Its job is to promote the event through dogged hard work, using the personal touch. Members of this committee spend hours on the phone talking up the event, inviting people to attend, selling tickets, helping find sponsors, and asking for favors. These people should have a wide circle of community contacts, especially among members of the target audience. They need to be skillful at securing the cooperation of others, and they should be strongly motivated to get the job done.

Public relations committee activities should be coordinated with the institution's public relations staff to maximize impact and to avoid stepping on toes. These committee members must also work with the powerful word-of-mouth grassroots networks that exist on every campus and in every community.

Gaining grassroots support and tapping into informal information networks can make an event take off. To accomplish this, get the attention of opinion leaders who can endorse the event with their constituents, and meet with them one-on-one to ask for their support.

Determine how information is channeled through the informal network, and then figure out how to make it work for you. Each group of people has its own network. To gain faculty support, you may need to get the endorsement of the deans; for students, working through the Greek system leaders may be key to success. In town, spread the word through community service organizations, or explain the event plans to business leaders over lunch.

Utilize no-cost ways to display the message, such as placing posters on bulletin boards on campus and around town in restaurants, churches, and other places where people gather. Use free listings in community affairs calendars published by newspapers, announced on local radio, and publicized by chambers of commerce and some churches.

Seek the help of merchants by asking to use their outdoor advertising message signs or their store display windows. Banks and utilities will sometimes allow promotional inserts to be mailed with their bills. Begin working with the campus "underground" before you need it. Never underestimate its power to make or break you.

• • •

Paid Advertising

Most events planners agree that paid advertising is one of the least successful ways to build attendance. Avoid using paid ads unless you are promoting a concert or entertainer to the general public and success depends upon selling out a large auditorium or convocation center.

Paid advertising is expensive, and you will be wasting your money if your ads don't reach your target audience. If you don't know how to buy ads, consult an advertising faculty member on campus or recruit an advertising professional to serve as a volunteer on your committee.

Save money on advertising by looking for a sponsor who will pay for the ads or by buying newspaper ads at a reduced rate on a "space available" basis. This means the ad will run, space permitting, usually within two weeks to one month. There is no guarantee when or even if the ad will appear—risky business if you must reach a specific market.

Outdoor advertising (billboards) is expensive but, depending on the location you purchase and the event you are promoting, it can be very effective. Ask for a nonprofit rate, which is similar to buying space-available newspaper ads. In outdoor advertising, the discount rate will pay for a certain number of billboards in a geographic area. Messages are posted where the company has unsold space within that area. Often these are not premier locations. The other catch: If a full-price purchaser wants the billboard where your message is posted, your sign comes down whether it has been up for one month or one day. If you do plan to purchase advertising, remember to include the expense in your event budget.

• • •

PSAs

Public service advertising (PSAs) donated by the media to nonprofit organizations is not a good tool for event promotion. Again, there is no guarantee that your announcement will be used. PSAs include radio announcements, drop-in ads that newspapers use to fill space, and television video spots that are used to fill odd bits of time. PSAs have to be professionally prepared and ready for use, thus adding costs to the budget, even though the ads may never make it off the shelf.

If your budget compels you to rely on PSAs, the best insurance for getting them used is to build a personal relationship with someone at the station or paper you intend to approach. So doing may help your announcement find its way to the top of the pile for airing at a prime time (instead of in the middle of the night). Another approach is to offer the media something desirable that they can promote as a giveaway. Radio stations like to promote things like free concert tickets to be won by listeners who call in.

• • •

Publicity Stunts

One technique that should be used cautiously and infrequently is the publicity stunt. Intended to generate photos or television footage that piques interest in an event, stunts must be offbeat, but not too crazy or offensive. For example, students building a mile-long ice cream sundae to call attention to a charitable fund-raising project would be a full-fledged stunt that merited notifying the media in advance.

On the other hand, the college president smoothing the last batch of concrete on the walk into a new building to call attention to the dedication ceremonies could more accurately be termed a publicity shot and does not warrant an invitation to the media. Instead, have the campus photographer take the photo and mail it to the media with an accompanying cutline or release and an invitation to attend formal dedication ceremonies.

Before agreeing to a stunt, remember that the personality of the stunt must match the personality of the event. Always check legal ramifications of stunts, particularly those that pose a risk of physical harm.

• • •

Media Parties

A media party before an event can be an effective tool for developing interest. Such functions are particularly useful for providing sneak previews of new facilities, art collections, scientific discoveries, and theatrical performances. The media party is intended for members of the broadcast and print media in the hope that they will convey your story in a favorable light. There are, however, no guarantees.

Determine your message, decide on the most appropriate media outlets for your news, and send media representatives an official invitation. Plan to supply good food and drink and, if necessary, accommodations. Media parties can take the form of an open house, a hard-hat inspection, or an exclusive showing. They can provide time for members of the press to try out a product or facility—such as spending a day working out in the new student recreation center or viewing the exhibits in the new gallery.

Amid the fun of a press party, be sure to deliver your message and plan to distribute press kits. A souvenir of the event imprinted with the special event logo is appropriate, but do not give expensive gifts or special privileges that could be construed as an attempt to "buy" the support of a reporter.

Realize that a reporter's job is to report the news objectively, so don't be surprised if the publicity generated by a media party contains a mix of compliment and criticism.

• • •

News Conferences

On certain occasions, a news conference may be an important component of an overall publicity plan. News conferences should be reserved for hard news, and credibility is key. Never call a news conference unless you have real news to announce. The idea of a news conference is to provide a forum for the delivery of important announcements that are considered breaking news. The news conference gives all media an equal opportunity to hear and report the news.

Telephone invitations to a news conference a day or two ahead. Try to schedule the conference for a mid-morning (10 or 11 a.m.) on a Tuesday, Wednesday, or Thursday. Mid-morning gives the evening newspaper and television news programs time to use your story that day. If you hold an afternoon news conference, try to do so at 1 or 2 p.m.; anything after 3 p.m. probably won't make the 5 or 6 p.m. news. Midweek days are preferable so that your story doesn't sit over a weekend.

The press room should be large and well-lit, with plenty of electrical outlets. Select a room on the first floor that is easy to find, with close parking so that camera crews don't have to struggle to haul heavy cameras and large tripods long distances and up stairways. You will need audio feeds (places to plug in audio) in large auditoriums. Work with the venue's technical staff on lighting and to send a signal from the microphone to a mixer where others can plug in for a feed.

Position the person to be interviewed in front of a backdrop, such as your institution's logo, and have a table for microphones and tape recorders in front of the podium. Have chairs arranged theater-style, and allow an aisle at least five feet wide in the back of the room, preferably with a riser, for television crews.

A press conference must have an agenda with a specified beginning and ending time. Included on the schedule should be a brief introduction of the featured speakers, the speaker's announcement or remarks, and a question-and-answer period. Respect media deadlines and keep the news conference on schedule.

Have refreshments such as coffee and soft drinks available in the room.

Supply a media kit—a packet of prepared information that reporters can use as background in preparing their stories. The kit should contain a news release and a copy of the remarks or speech made during the press conference, along with some general information about the institution and biographical information on the speaker. Include a copy of the event program; biographies and pictures of principal speakers, honored guests, and VIPs; a copy of citations that will be read; information about event sponsors and members of the event planning committee; and the names and telephone numbers of institution or public relations officials to contact for more information. Resist the temptation to create an expensive, slick media kit stuffed with extraneous information. In truth, many reporters would prefer a simple one-page fact sheet that answers who, what, when, where, how, why, and so what to a fancy folder filled with things they don't have time to read.

If possible, have a quiet, private room ready for reporters to conduct in-depth interviews at the conclusion of the news conference.

There are several potential drawbacks to holding a news conference. First, poor attendance on the part of the media is embarrassing and makes it appear that your news is not important. Second, the media can grill your VIP and then generate stories that are very different from what you had envisioned. Third, the media representatives may decide that your event isn't really news and that a news conference wasn't necessary. Unfortunately, after this kind of credibility-damaging experience, attendance at your next news conference is likely to be light.

• • •

The Press Room

Special events that feature a number of dignitaries, celebrities, and attractions may require a press room.

A press room serves as headquarters for the media on campus. It should be easily accessible, centrally located, and staffed at all times. The press room should contain telephones; telephone jacks for computers; sufficient electrical outlets for plugging in computers and other devices; fax machines; all tickets, badges, and identification needed for admission to events; photos, releases, and copies of speeches; and background information on all speakers and honored guests.

There should be a separate, quiet room available for interviews as well as a staff of eager messengers ready to shuttle people to and from events and to deliver messages from editors' desks to reporters on assignment. Journalism students are usually delighted to serve as messengers in exchange for the experience of associating with the working media.

Good media coverage correlates closely with whether or not reporters had a good experience covering the event. The event PR committee can help make it as easy as possible for reporters to do their jobs.

Working with the campus public relations staff, members of the PR committee can help guide the press during the event. The PR office should brief committee members and give them specific assignments. Those stationed near the door can greet media representatives, lead them to important people, make introductions, help set up photos, and provide event background information. Members should know the order of the program and the layout of the facility so that they can direct reporters to telephones or to a quiet spot to conduct an interview.

Anything that can be done to make the event and its stars more accessible will improve and increase coverage and make reporters enthusiastic about attending future events at your institution.

Be sure to do these, too:

- Invite the media to your event (don't assume they know they are welcome) and provide them with good seats.
- Send your news to the wire services.
- Call reporters when you think you have news they can use or when you want to encourage coverage from particular reporters.
- Make faculty experts available to the media to comment on special events and to provide background information for stories.
- Offer to arrange interviews and photos.
- Hire a professional photographer to cover the event. You can use photos as keepsake gifts for volunteers, as publicity for next year's event, in follow-up news releases, and in internal media such as the alumni magazine. Many planners prepare scrapbooks of events to be presented to corporate sponsors, honorary degree or award recipients, and other VIP guests.
- Before the event, determine the purpose for the photos and meet with the photographer to discuss the kind of photos you want, how you plan to use them, and whether they should be in color, black and white, or a combination. Give him or her a list of specific shots to take. Assign a PR committee member or a staff member who knows the guests to guide the photographer and to record the names of people in specific photos.
- An award-winning campus photographer suggests improving the quality of photos by arranging to take VIP pictures before or after the event. That way, the photographer can plan the lighting and background and spend enough time with the subjects to capture them at their best. Numerous shots can be taken instead of relying on a one-chance photo. Avoid

photographing people sitting in meetings or speakers at podiums, tables covered with dirty dishes, and guests holding drinks. Ask people to remove name badges before pictures are taken.

- In preparation for the event, give photographers the invitation, a list of people and topics to be photographed, the address of the facility, and phone numbers in case of a problem. Tell the photographer the dress so that he or she can blend in and feel comfortable. Planners should tell other staff members that photography has been arranged in advance so that colleagues don't try to direct the photographer during the event. Impromptu photos waste time and can run up expenses. Photographers should be afforded the same privileges as the rest of the staff. If you feed the staff, feed the photographer.

• • •

Follow Up

As with every other aspect of event planning, publicity requires follow-up. Reporters who covered the event appreciate a note of thanks for their efforts. You should also evaluate which publicity techniques worked and which did not. Write an evaluation with suggestions for future events and put it in the events file.

CHAPTER 3

Find a Place, Get Comfortable

THE FACILITY YOU CHOOSE CAN MAKE OR break an event. Use your imagination to choose a facility that will advance your theme and provide additional incentive to attend. Take advantage of the lure of a place that is not open to the general public. An invitation to the president's home is a draw on most campuses. So is an invitation to a grand private home or club. Give routine meetings a breath of fresh air by serving lunch out-of-doors in pretty baskets. One university climaxes reunion weekend with a Sunset Dinner and Moonlight Dance held on the inner quad.

For some special events, facilities are the raison d'etre. A fund-raiser to build a new savannah for the zoo's African animals could appropriately be held outdoors after hours at the zoo.

When choosing a facility, think first of the purpose of your gathering. Obviously, the needs are quite different for a workshop where every participant will use a personal computer than they are for an art festival. Make a list of facilities on your campus and in your area that might meet your needs; then do some legwork.

Schedule an appointment and visit each site. Ask the facility's manager about capacity for the type of function you are considering (the same room can hold more people for a stand-up reception than for a sit-down dinner); what auxiliary services are available; and what provisions need to be made for food service, parking, and security. Some places require that you use their personnel and services; others have none available, and still others have a list of approved vendors from which you must choose. Ask about rental rates, availability, and time for setup if you need it. Be certain to see the rooms you will actually be using, not a "sample" or "typical" room. Initiating a face-to-face relationship with the facility manager and staff will also help you get better service as you go through the planning and execution of your event.

Each facility has a personality conducive to certain types of events. Don't try to stage an elegant black-tie gala in a broken-down gymnasium. By the same token, don't invite guests to the country club and serve a luncheon of jumbo shrimp and imported wine when you are trying to communicate the university's budget crisis.

Remember that the tone of your event—the setting and presentation—must be consistent with its purpose. Don't undercut your message with confusing inconsistencies.

When you visit a facility, try to picture it as your guests will see it and at the time of day or night they will be using it. How does it look from the outside? What style is conveyed by the decor? Do the meeting rooms have windows? If so, what will your guests see?

We once held a one-day executive retreat to discuss some very serious issues. The site was a renovated Victorian mansion in the heart of a large city. Everything was strictly first-class—the grounds, the interior, the meeting rooms, the food, and service. But, unfortunately, several "hourly hotels" lined the other side of the street, and the "ladies" were much in evidence. As our guests arrived, everyone made mention of the women. By lunchtime, jokes about them dotted conversation to the point of distraction. When our guests look back on this event, I'm sure they remember the presence of those women more than any feature of that facility.

If you are in the habit of using the same campus facility over and over again, perhaps you should take a fresh look at it before holding your next event there. Visit the facility and look at it as if you were a guest on a first visit. Is the route from the parking lot to the front door clean and pleasant? Is the name of the building clearly visible? Are pathways and directions plainly marked? Is there a receptionist or an easy-to-decipher directory inside the front door? Do graffiti, litter, or tattered furniture clutter the hallways?

Are the rooms clean, the furniture in good repair, the air fresh? Sit on the chairs. Is the light adequate for reading? Check the air conditioning for drafts. Your guests will be sitting or standing at your function in that room, in those chairs, with that lighting: Would you be comfortable doing what you will be asking your guests to do?

What feeling do you get from the room? Is it dark and depressing or attractive and properly lit? Does everything work? Can it comfortably accommodate your group? Find out what other groups will be using the facility that same day and if they are compatible. We once inadvertently planned an alumni college for the same week as a high school cheerleading camp. By the week's end, our middle-aged participants had learned countless new cheers—at all hours of the day and night.

• • •

Make a Silk Purse

Scratched dishes, battered flatware, worn furnishings, and less-than-perfect walls are facts of life for most campus event planners. When you are talking about repeatedly using the same campus rooms, it is worth the time and minimal expense to implement a few tricks to fool the eye.

The easiest and least expensive way to disguise flaws is with lighting. Install dimmer switches so that light levels can be adjusted according to the function.

Changing the wattage or color of bulbs can also produce a softer look or more flattering color. Another technique is to place theater gels over lights. (Don't tape the gels directly on the lights; instead, enlist the help of your theater department to use gels safely.)

When working in a gymnasium, define your space with borrowed halogen floor lamps that shoot light upward. Position the lamps around the perimeter of the space you are featuring, and connect them to power with extension cords.

At dinner, set the mood with lots of candles. Save money by purchasing small, inexpensive tea lights instead of votive candles if you need them for only one function. A tea light will burn for about the length of a dinner party and will fit in most votive cups or an assortment of improvised holders. (Be sure the container is fireproof.)

Are walls the problem? An uninviting room is often the victim of a bad paint job, and one of the easiest ways to alter a room's mood is to change the wall color. Before repainting, study the room at different times of day to observe light conditions, and use your observations to help select a better color.

When you can't repaint, hide problem areas or unattractive features with fabric. Borrow a decorative screen, make your own, or tack lengths of fabric over the unsightly area. Conceal tacks by using a hot-glue gun to attach cord or braid over them.

• • •

Unusual Settings

Inject some imagination into the selection of the setting for your event. Perhaps the facility you have chosen has a beautiful garden. Maybe there is a spot on campus with a particularly attractive view, or perhaps there is a pleasant room not usually used for entertaining that could be transformed for that purpose.

But to avoid unpleasant surprises, always make a site visit and thoroughly talk through your ideas with the person in charge. I once staged an elegant candlelight reception following a performance by a rising opera star. It was the first time we used the choral rehearsal room for entertaining. We incorporated the musical instruments, music stands, and chairs normally stored in the room as part of our theme. The grand piano became one of the decorating focal points. Things went beautifully until guests began setting their empty champagne flutes and dirty plates on the piano. This greatly agitated the music department administrator, and his comments embarrassed several of our guests. The situation could have been avoided if I had had a more thorough discussion with him before planning to use the room.

Scheduling events in unusual places offers both pros and cons. On the positive side, the event will be more interesting and novel and therefore will remain in people's memories far longer. On the negative side, when you schedule an event for an unusual place, you substantially increase the chances that mistakes will occur and unexpected things will go wrong.

Questions to ask yourself

Ask yourself a few questions before committing to an unusual spot:

- Does the location make sense? Does it support your goals, and will it make a positive impression?
- Can you afford to budget for the additional costs of moving the necessary equipment and staff to the location?
- If outdoors, could weather or insects become a factor? If it rains, do you have an alternative facility readily available? How would you notify guests of such a change?
- Can the caterer do a good job in that location? If there is no provision for electricity or water, you may have problems.
- If you are planning an evening event, how will you light the area?
- Is the area secure?
- Is there parking nearby? Are there restroom facilities?
- Do your plans comply with applicable fire codes and regulations concerning consumption of alcoholic beverages?
- Do you need any special permits?
- Will your insurance cover you at the site?

Events in tents

Looking for a place to hold commencement luncheon or class reunions? Need to seat 800 people for the president's inauguration luncheon? Do you require a hospitality facility for a major athletic event? How about renting a tent?

Modern tents bear little resemblance to the dusty canvas shelters many of us recall from the county fair. In some cases, today's tents are nicer than many permanent spaces.

Tents come in a variety of shapes, colors, and sizes and with accessories that afford all the comforts of being indoors. Liners, lighting, flooring, heating, and air conditioning are all possibilities. Entrances can be built to include real doors; sides can feature windows; and covered walkways can guide guests from one venue to another. The only limits are your creativity and budget.

Start by discussing your needs, ideas, and budget with the rental company early in the planning process.

The first thing to know is where the tent will be set up. Is the surface a lawn, parking lot, patio, or deck? This is important because it may dictate what type of tent is needed.

There are three main types of tents in use today: pole tents that rely on a system of internal center poles and external guy lines attached to stakes pounded into the ground; frame tents, which can stand by themselves and which use guy lines attached to weights instead of stakes; and clearspan tents, which have no interior poles but instead are supported by an aluminum frame.

Each type has advantages and disadvantages. Pole tents are the least expensive but require a minimum of eight feet of clearance around the perimeter to accommodate the guy lines and stakes. Frame tents are excellent for extending a room because they can stand by themselves. Stability comes from guy lines attached to stakes or anchored to weights such as barrels that are each filled with 750 pounds of water or cement. Clearspan tents are the most steady for areas where inclement weather may be a factor and are ideal for occasions when guests need an unobstructed view. They are also the most expensive.

The rental company can figure the correct size tent based on the number of people you will be hosting and the activities involved. Figure about six square feet per person and six-foot-wide aisles for a theater-style setup. For a served dinner, figure 12 square feet per person. For dancing, you will need four-and-a-half square feet per person. Stages, buffets, bars and other large items also need to be factored in.

Although tent renters will bid on large jobs (like a multiday festival requiring several tents), most companies have set prices and don't dicker. Contracts usually require a 25-percent deposit, with the balance due the day the tent is put up. Suppliers like to set up several days ahead to allow for the chance of bad weather. Setup for a Saturday event may take place on Wednesday. This gives the crew two days and leaves at least one day for decorating and load-in of equipment. The tent would likely be taken down on Monday.

Before contracting for a tent, check local codes and permit requirements, which vary according to state, county and city laws, and fire codes. Usually, securing a permit requires showing the rental company's fire-retardant certificate; explaining your layout, especially the location and number of exits; and paying a fee than can range from $25 to $100.

The planner is also responsible for having the site ready before the setup crew arrives. This includes marking the locations of underground utilities including gas, telephone, and cable TV lines (call local utilities in advance for this service) and removing any obstacles from the area (such as cars parked in the lot you intend to use.)

One way to make a tent look extra-special is to use a liner. Liners are just what the name implies—fabric that lines the tent's interior to lend a fancy appearance or to hide the tent's skeleton or imperfections. There are three common types: flat, pleated, and balloon.

Flat liners simply provide a smooth surface on the tent's interior, while pleated liners make a series of arching lines leading to the top of the tent. Balloon liners create a flowing, billowy effect.

Liners usually come in white and are installed by the tent company. While liners deliver the look of polished sophistication, they can double the cost of the tent.

A budget-conscious alternative is to camouflage the tent's inner workings by hanging fire-retardant colored ribbon or strips of mylar or fabric.

For some occasions you may want to consider adding a floor. Tent flooring works best on flat surfaces such as a parking lot. The most economical system creates a floor with interlocking plastic components. It comes in a variety of colors and is designed to drain away spills. Another popular type, called "lay-down decking," consists of sheets of plywood.

A common misunderstanding about flooring is that it will be level. In truth, flooring will follow the contours of whatever is underneath.

Level floors are very expensive because they have to be custom engineered and built for the site. They must conform to city codes about weight bearing because they are a suspended surface.

Lighting sets the mood, and today's tents can dazzle with track lighting, dimmers, miniature string lights, pole lights with colored gels, and chandeliers. If your tent rental company does not have these products, rent them from a lighting specialty firm. Coordinate with the tent company to be certain enough supports are in place to handle the weight of anything that will be hung from the ceiling.

Too chilly? Guests' feet can be toasty warm on cool days if you rent propane heaters. If your guests are too hot, cooling them off is also possible, but pricey. Air conditioning can be installed, but the job must be subcontracted to an air-conditioning professional.

Most tent companies are insured if a natural occurrence (like a severe storm) damages the tent. Their insurance will not cover your possessions. Check with your risk-management office to determine if you are adequately covered. Security for a tent is the renter's responsibility.

• • •

The Setup

As a special event planner, you will be involved with many different types of functions. Each requires a setup, an arrangement of furniture and props that will provide maximum comfort for your guests and best fulfill the purpose of your event. A hotel catering manager observed that she thinks people take the room arrangement too lightly, noting that it is the first impression people have of the event. Yet many planners treat it casually or misunderstand hotel technology and wind up with the wrong setup. A good setup should facilitate crowd flow, complement the venue you have chosen, and make the most of decorations. Determining the setup requires going to the room to see what is there and arranging and rearranging the furniture, at least on paper if not physically.

Computer software is available to make this task easier. Most programs begin by asking you for room dimensions. The program then scales furnishings to the appropriate size and keeps them in proportion no matter how many times you rearrange. Room setup software typically offers shapes including rectangle, round, square, and banquet tables; audiovisual equipment such as screens, overheads, slide projectors, cameras, and microphones; specialty items like pipe and drape, pianos, plants, bars, doors, posts, and columns; dance floors; and staging. The software takes the guesswork out of calculating how many people and furnishings will fit into a room. Instead of a hasty sketch, planners can work from a precisely scaled layout that shows everything from exits and electrical outlets to furnishings and dance floors. This flexibility means you can plan an alumni event under tents in the chancellor's backyard, right down to the position of the tent posts. Room setup software may yield the greatest benefit when you can't be on site to supervise. Setup crews will know exactly what you have in mind when you give them printed room diagrams drawn to scale and detailed inventory reports of the required equipment.

Get started deciding which arrangement you want by seeking the advice of the staff at the facility you have chosen. These people have seen many groups come and go and can offer ideas and suggestions to help you achieve the best setup for the needs of your particular function.

Consider the sequence of events during your function. Do people need to be able to move freely from one place to another? A common mistake is situating registration tables or bars in places where they create a bottleneck or block traffic. Locate these stations so that people can come and go easily. An enticing display, entertainment, or a reception line placed on the opposite side of the room will help keep traffic moving.

Think about what you are expecting guests to do during the function. I once attended a charity auction where the items to be sold were displayed on long tables. Unfortunately, the tables were so close together that it was impossible to examine items and place bids. As a result, many bids were lost because people simply weren't willing to fight the crowd. Another technique for keeping knots from forming is to have a receptionist at a registration table greet guests and then direct them to another locale immediately. Try placing welcoming foods such as coffee and rolls well away from registration tables.

The setup should maximize the beauty of the facility and give a neat, well-organized appearance. If you have been forced to use a room that is much too large, divide it with portable screens, pipe and drape, or large potted plants. This will help avoid the impression that your event is not well attended.

Hotels and conference facilities use formulas based on particular setup styles to calculate seating capacities for each room. These figures represent the maximum capacity and don't provide for space lost to head tables, audiovisual equipment, displays, or registration tables. Consider the capacity provided by the site's staff, but remember to take into account the special needs of your event.

To maximize catering profits, hotels and banquet halls rely on a glove-like fit of people to space. Don't expect a facility manager to assign a room that is far more spacious than what is dictated by the number of guests you are expecting—unless you are willing to pay extra for it. Although hotels sometimes do not charge for the room itself—as they make their money principally from food and beverage service—you should expect to pay a rental or at least a setup fee for each room you use.

Here are some guidelines for calculating capacity for common setups.

Theater or auditorium style

This is probably the most commonly used setup for lectures and speakers. Chairs are arranged in rows facing a podium. Plan to leave two four-foot aisles, a 5-foot center aisle, and a five-foot front aisle so that people can get in and out easily. Be certain that the people in the back row can see and hear. If there is any doubt, place the podium or speaker's table on a riser and arrange for a good sound system.

To calculate the number of people who can fit into a theater-style room, multiply the length of the room by its width and divide by seven to get maximum capacity, including aisle space.

Classroom style

This is the most desirable setup for meetings where participants will be required to sit for long periods and to take notes. Tables and chairs are arranged in rows facing a speaker's table or podium. It is most comfortable to have a center aisle and not more than three people per six-foot banquet table (two is better). The drawback to this setup is that is requires a large room and uses a lot of space, and occasionally it involves an additional charge. To find seating capacity for classroom setups, multiply the length of the room by its width and divide by 17. This will give you maximum capacity if you use meeting tables that are 18 inches wide and six or eight feet long. If the tables are 30 inches wide, divide by 23.

Board or conference style

Tables are set up to form a solid rectangle with chairs around the perimeter. Sometimes this shape will be rounded off on each end with half-moon-shaped tables. The number of people who can be accommodated by this setup varies greatly with the style of chairs you are using. As you will probably use this setup to accommodate a small group of important people who need to be able to see, hear, and talk to one another, pay close attention to comfort. Chairs should be spaced so that participants can turn and get in and out of their seats without bumping the person next to them.

"T," "E," and "U" shapes

Common for groups of less than 40, these configurations are all based on an arrangement of six- or eight-foot tables with chairs placed around the outside edges. "T" and "U" shapes are good for meetings where people need to interact with a discussion leader or to see a demonstration. The "E" shape is sometimes used for meals, but it wastes a lot of space, and the people seated on the back of the "E" are forced to stare at the sides of the heads of the people on the inside of the "E." None of these shapes is suitable for audiovisual presentations.

Moving reception

This is sometimes called a "stand-up" reception because guests are not seated. People mingle as they serve themselves food from a buffet or several food stations and get beverages from a bar. The number of people who can be accommodated by this arrangement is largely dictated by the fire capacity set by local ordinances. Be careful, however, not to stuff the room. Not only are guests uncomfortable having to squeeze by one another, but an overly full room makes it difficult for the hosts to greet guests and for people to reach food and beverage areas. You can figure capacity for a moving reception by multiplying the length of the room by its width and dividing by seven.

When you are planning food stations, bars, and displays, keep tables away from the main doors and be careful not to block fire exits. Distribute foods to different stations for interest and variety. One table could hold cheese and fruit, one hot hors d'oeuvres, one sweets. When expecting a large crowd, have several bars and make a separate serving station for people who do not want mixed drinks. A punch table or soda bar cuts down on the traffic jam and eliminates frustration for people who want nonalcoholic beverages.

Banquet style

For meal service for a large group of people, this setup typically uses 60-inch round tables, which comfortably seat eight or 10 people. Multiply the length of the room by its width and divide by 10 to determine the maximum number of guests. This allows for a four-and-one-half-foot aisle between tables. If you are planning to have a head table, eliminate one entire row of tables. Before deciding to seat 10 people at each table, carefully consider your function. If there are many courses, wine and champagne glasses at each place, a large centerpiece, and several sauces or condiments, it is preferable to seat only eight people per table to avoid crowding plates and glasses. If guests will be wearing formal attire, seating eight people at each table is a much more gracious arrangement.

One problem with the round-table setup is that at least two guests per table will have to turn completely around to see the dais. If table and room space permit, you can set each table for eight. Two places (without chairs or a place setting) toward the speaker are left open. A low centerpiece or other decoration as well as rolls and condiments can be arranged attractively in this space. While this setup somewhat reduces the conversation options and increases the "passing" responsibilities of the guests nearest the open space, it may be the best arrangement if the after-meal program is lengthy or includes audiovisuals.

• • •

The Dance Floor

The arrangement of the dance floor varies greatly with the room, the program, and how many of the guests will actually dance. For a dinner dance, avoid arranging a large dance floor in the center of a ballroom with tables at each end; when guests are seated for dinner, the large empty space in the room's center makes it seem as though two separate functions are in progress with the dance floor in between.

• • •

Setting Up the Setups

If you are conducting a conference or seminar, you probably will be using several rooms for different sessions over the course of the day. As you plan for setups, try to restrict yourself to one basic arrangement for each room and do not attempt to reset the rooms between sessions. Putting up and taking down tables, chairs, and other equipment takes considerable time and often makes a good deal of noise that can disrupt sessions in other rooms. Here are some more tips:

- Test all audiovisual equipment before the first session.
- Water pitchers should be refilled and dirty glasses picked up during breaks and between sessions.

• • •

Setup Checklist

Here are some details to check before your guests arrive:

- Check for wobbly table legs, and be sure that folding legs are locked into position.
- Chairs must be clean, with legs that sit evenly on the floor.
- Table skirting should be firmly attached so that it is not inadvertently pulled down when guests are seated.
- Check for obstructed views.
- The sound system must allow everyone to hear but not blast them out. No one should be seated right in front of a large speaker.
- Look for torn or stained linen, and be certain replacements are available.
- Make sure all place settings include the full complement of glasses and silverware and that it is all clean and spot-free.
- Check placecards against your seating chart.
- Check that each table has favors, programs, and menu cards.

• • •

The Dais

The dais, sometimes referred to as the head table, is a raised platform at one end of the room for honored guests, VIPs, speakers, and those instrumental to the success of a function. Although I prefer to eliminate the dais whenever possible, if you do use one, check it carefully for appearance and safety. Additional concerns:

- The dais table should be covered with a floor-length skirt.
- The riser should be wide enough for participants to push their chairs back and stand without fear of toppling off.
- Steps leading to the dais should be sturdy and not too steep and narrow. A railing is a good idea.
- Floral arrangements or candles should not block the faces of the dais guests. Check this by sitting at one of the banquet tables on the main floor and looking up.
- Cords for microphones and other audiovisual equipment should be taped to the floor.

- Turn on and pretest all electrical equipment, including the podium light and microphone.
- Place each speaker's notes in a file folder with his or her name marked in large letters on the outside. Stack the folders in order from first speaker to last. This is especially helpful for avoiding mixups during award presentation ceremonies.
- Have a glass for each speaker and a small pitcher of water in an inconspicuous place near the podium.

• • •

Checkrooms and Restrooms

Whenever you are entertaining guests, you should provide a secure place to store their coats, umbrellas, and other personal items. An attended checkroom is essential for formal occasions where some guests may have fur coats. If you use a checkroom that is open to other guests at the facility, request that there will be sufficient checkroom staff on duty to meet your needs and prevent long lines. For extra special occasions, such as a black-tie capital campaign kick-off, arrange to have the costs of your guests' coat checks added to your master account. Make sure you include this cost in your event budget.

If there is not a checkroom in the facility, you can create one in a storage room or a large area under a stairwell or some other convenient place. Borrow or rent portable coat racks and make numbered claim tickets. Checkrooms do not have to be accessible to guests. A team of student hosts and hostesses can take coats as guests arrive, hang them in out-of-the-way closets, and retrieve them as guests leave. Assign someone to stay with the coats at all times. Check your insurance to be certain you are covered in the event of a loss.

Immaculately clean, completely stocked restrooms are an important behind-the-scenes element. Check all restrooms just before guests arrive and periodically during the event. Schedule housekeeping to clean and restock throughout the event and encourage good service by tipping them generously.

When you are hosting an elegant affair at a facility with Spartan amenities, place tissues, fresh flowers, and some pretty soap in the restrooms.

Dignitaries and celebrities should be provided access to a private restroom, preferably with a quiet sitting area where they can have privacy.

• • •

Decor

Decorations express the theme and set the tone for a memorable occasion. Decor refers to everything from tabletop floral arrangements to theater-style lighting to "flats," props, costumes, and music. Decor is the creation of that little bit of magic that communicates your theme and tells guests your event is truly special.

One university hosted a seminar on Latin America and its likely role in the 21st century. Planners used decor to stimulate all the senses.

- The Saturday event was attended by 200 people and began with a Brazilian breakfast of crab soufflé, homemade tamales, and an array of tropical fruits. Butterflies and lush greenery decorated the room while the recorded sounds of tropical birds and rainforest waterfalls played in the background.
- The morning included a conversation with the university president, a faculty member's presentation on Mexican fiestas, and faculty roundtables on topics ranging from geology to politics.
- A professional dancer presented a class on rumba and tango.
- At lunchtime, participants tried Caribbean cuisine including jerk chicken, fried plantains, black beans, and ginger beer. Tropical birds and flowers were part of the decor, and the sounds of reggae music completed the atmosphere.
- A black-tie dinner and program at a hotel ended the day. Guests were greeted by a classical guitarist and a performing troupe of exotic birds. Handlers dressed in black tie circulated with the birds in the reception area. Guests could pet and hold the birds and have photos taken with them. Photos were then mailed to guests as an event follow-up.
- A four-course dinner featured the cuisine of Chile, Peru, and Argentina and included baked scallops, filet mignon with ancho chili sauce, and shell-shaped gingersnap cups with pineapple mousse and fresh mango.
- Custom-made linens of copper-colored silk and fuschia-colored cotton covered the tables. Centerpieces were copper- and fuschia-colored flowers with black Spanish fans. Gold and fuschia gels were put in lighting sockets to create a dramatic effect.
- Entertainment was provided by a professional Latin American dance team performing the tango, cha-cha, bolero, samba, and rumba.

Universities are at an advantage when it comes to creating fabulous decor on very little budget. The resources, talents, and know-how of students and faculty in the theater, art, and music departments are an excellent source of inspiration and help.

Work with the university grounds crew to grow the plants and flowers you will need throughout the year. Recruit volunteers to make favors, tie ribbons on napkins, letter placecards, and arrange flowers.

There are also many vendors who rent everything from props to linen, fancy glasses and china. Check the Yellow Pages under "party rentals."

Here are some additional decor tips:

- Plan decor early, and work in advance to avoid a last-minute panic.
- Enlist a volunteer who has a vendor's license to purchase flowers wholesale. Recruit someone from the art department or another volunteer to arrange them for you.
- Build an inventory of decorating staples to avoid repeatedly renting them. Buy simple candleholders, a supply of baskets that can be used for centerpieces with pots of seasonal flowers, and plain vases and floral

arrangement bases. (Secondhand stores are a great place to find these at very little cost. Not in the color or shapes you want? Vases and baskets can be spray-painted, and the shapes don't have to be identical.)

- Invest in a quantity of seasonal dried arrangements that can be used repeatedly. An autumn arrangement can work from the beginning of school until the holidays. Share the costs with another office, such as the president's office. After one season, take the arrangements apart and salvage as many pieces as possible, but don't save the arrangements from year to year—they get too bedraggled.
- Save florist's bows and ribbons. Streamers can be ironed and reused.
- Keep a list of people who like to sew, make crafts, paint, do calligraphy, and arrange flowers and call them to help early in the planning process.
- Pick up ideas at local crafts fairs. Part-time or home-based craftspeople often can create customized items at a considerable savings over commercial shops.

• • •

Equipment Sources

Almost any decorating or party accessory can be rented, from pinatas to snow-cone machines. Explore the possibilities. For items in limited supply or great demand (such as tents for spring weekends), reserve well in advance. Make sure you know the payment policy of the rental firm—many require a check at the time of delivery, even for institutional customers. Inspect the equipment carefully to make sure that everything is in good condition and that the correct number was delivered.

A school, college, or university often has a broad array of equipment available within the institution. For example, many have silver services stashed in a trophy case or locked in a closet in the president's office. As you uncover these treasures, keep a list on file, including contacts and procedures for using the equipment.

If you have your own facility where most of your organization's special events take place, it makes sense, in the long run, to purchase frequently rented equipment such as these:

- flatware;
- china;
- serving pieces;
- coffee urns;
- sugars and creamers;
- chafing dishes;
- pitchers for coffee and water;
- water goblets;
- wineglasses for white wine, red wine, and champagne;
- round tables for eight to 10 people; and
- stacking chairs, upholstered in a neutral color and suitable for dining and conferences.

• • •

Security

Security isn't just guarding coats in the checkroom and preventing outsiders from crashing your party. If you are planning a large function or an outdoor event, you will need to provide security for crowd and traffic control as well as to ensure the safety of any celebrities who may be participating.

Begin security planning early in the development of your event. As soon as the date is selected and type of event is determined, meet with campus security or the security people at an off-campus facility. If necessary, they will coordinate arrangements with local police.

Security officers need to know how many people are expected, the nature of the event, and the schedule of activities. They should be informed of the presence of celebrities or others who may require escorts. Police officers should handle parking, direct traffic, and control access to facilities.

When a gathering ends after dark, arrange to have patrols in parking lots, garages, and along routes where guests will be walking. Plan a security escort service to accompany single people to their cars.

On some campuses, the expense of security for special events is covered by the university. For others, the event sponsor is billed.

• • •

Where to Park?

Parking is a big problem whether events are held in city hotels, at civic buildings, or on campus. While definitely an unglamorous part of events management, parking is a critical concern that should be addressed early in planning. Lack of parking may even force reconsideration of a venue.

- Parking should be easily accessible, especially for night events. If the parking area or garage is too far away, arrange for a valet or shuttle-bus service.
- Check with your institution's risk management office about insurance coverages, particularly if you are using students or volunteers to park cars.
- Be sure the lots have adequate security, both while guests' cars are parked and for people walking to their cars. All parking areas should be well llit and patrolled.
- Always reserve places for guests of honor, campus officials, and anyone else who is crucial to your program.
- When using areas without marked parking places, such as a field or lawn, have people directing cars so that lines are straight, exits are clear, adequate driving lanes are available, and the maximum number of vehicles can be accommodated.
- Consider hiring a professional parking service to manage parking for large public events like festivals. These services post directional and no-parking

signs, provide attendants, and handle security and insurance.

- On campus, always try to provide free parking, even if it means building the costs into ticket prices and paying a lump sum from the event budget. Definitely provide VIP parking for event sponsors, underwriters, and patrons as one of the perks that go with higher priced tickets.
- Consider the weather and how it will affect your parking arrangements; determine when the majority of people will want to leave; and check other events that may be happening on campus at the same time.
- If you are reserving a parking lot for special use, post a notice a few days ahead so that people can make other arrangements. Secure the lots as early as possible to prevent unwanted parkers from filling spaces.
- How many spaces will you need? As a general rule, figure 2.5 people per car. Remember to provide handicapped parking and emergency access lanes for fire or other emergency vehicles. Campus security can advise you on your state's requirements.
- When planning an event on campus, meet with parking services or campus security early in the process. If you are sponsoring a large concert or festival in a convocation center or stadium, campus security will probably already have a plan for parking, lot security, and dispersing traffic. Critical to getting cars out of the lots is a plan that will enable traffic to flow away from the venue as quickly as possible. This can be accomplished by making clearly marked exits, providing adequate signage indicating which lanes to use to connect with major highways, and, when necessary, restricting traffic to one-way on key arteries.
- At some campus football stadiums, traffic is funneled into the stadium via one-way streets before kickoff. After the game, those same routes are reversed so that traffic flows one-way out. Campus security may also suggest stationing officers at the intersections of major roads in a two-block area to direct traffic and regulate traffic signals.
- It is a good idea to create a parking command post atop a building or on a scaffolding from which officers can see the big picture. People in the command post can use walkie-talkies to tell officers directing cars how best to regulate traffic.
- For smaller events—especially formal occasions—members of campus service clubs, athletic teams, or Greek organizations are usually happy to provide valet service in exchange for a contribution.
- If you plan to use students or to hire valets, check with your risk management office to determine any additional insurance needs. Meet with the valets before the event to discuss where and how to park the cars, what to wear, and when to report for work. Emphasize the need to respect the automobiles they will be driving.
- Establish a policy on tipping, and be sure the valets know and obey it.
- If you create a shuttle service, use enough vehicles to minimize waiting, especially at peak times. All vans and shuttles should be free of charge and

clearly marked. Provide each guest with information on routes, times, and stops. If you are short on vehicles, contact the local school district about renting buses.

- Many universities have a transportation department that can assist with arrangements or that may be available for hire. Although it may be the most expensive option, hiring regular university drivers is wise because they are already covered by the institution's insurance. If you must hire outside help, check state and local laws regulating who is eligible to drive vehicles for this purpose. In many states, anyone who drives a bus or van to transport a group of people must be at least 21 years old and have a chauffeur's license.
- Meet with shuttle drivers beforehand to review work schedules and routes and to discuss the event in detail. Review where to pick up passengers and how long to wait. Drivers will probably be your guests' first point of contact, and many visitors will ask them general questions. Leave activity schedules on each bus, and be certain the drivers are knowledgeable about not only the event but your campus and are willing to make a friendly impression.
- In a city, likely places to arrange satellite parking are shopping malls, buildings with private garages not in use after hours, and paid lots that are empty at night.
- Parking at public buildings like civic centers, theaters, music halls, and athletic stadiums is usually run by a different company from the one that manages the facility.
- Some rental contracts include parking, but in other cases it may be necessary to negotiate a separate parking agreement in addition to the facility rental agreement. If you don't want guests to pay for parking on arrival, make arrangements for vouchers or a lump payment based on the total number of cars parked.
- At hotels that have private garages, negotiate parking as part of your rental contract and try swapping parking for recognition in the event program, especially if the event is a fund raiser. (Note: Parking is not deductible as a gift-in-kind because it is a service.) If yours is a fund-raising event, consider giving parking vouchers for the hotel's garage to guests as they check in.
- If you are using a private country club or similar facility that has valet parking, negotiate the fees including a flat tip so that guests do not have to pay.
- If you want to offer VIPs special parking, arrange it in advance so that parking workers know where to direct cars.

Unfortunately, efforts to make guests feel welcome can sometimes irritate campus neighbors and employees. At one university, staffers are periodically displaced from their regular parking places without notice to accommodate guests attending a quarterly seminar sponsored by the conferences office. On seminar mornings, traffic jams result in an already-congested part of campus while angry regular parkers are turned away and forced to fend for themselves.

Another university's president's home is situated in an upscale neighborhood at the end of a cul-de-sac and lacks parking for all but a few cars. The home is frequently used for entertaining, and over the course of time neighbors grew weary of the eyesore and inconvenience of cars parked along the residential street. The neighbors got up a successful petition to prevent parking on the street. Cars are now valet-parked at a lot several blocks away.

If event parking or traffic frequently impinges on your neighbors, try improving relations by sending them a friendly note and a schedule of major events before each semester begins. Plan a gathering just for them once a year to say thanks for being such good sports.

CHAPTER 4

Eat, Drink, and Be Merry

FOOD AND BEVERAGES ARE AN INTEGRAL part of good hospitality, and good food and drink, imaginatively presented, go far toward creating the right ambiance. When event planners at the University of Virginia wanted to evoke the spirit of Thomas Jefferson for a capital campaign kickoff event, they researched and served dishes that were popular in his lifetime. Guests enjoyed smoked salmon, stuffed and grilled guinea fowl, Muscovy duck, Sally Lunn bread, and timbales of puréed peas and sweet potatoes. Dessert was pumpkin mousse.

Food and beverages will likely be the largest single expense for your event, so plan to devote adequate time to research and develop your offerings and to select a caterer who can execute plans deliciously and with flair.

When you first meet with your campus caterer or the catering manager at a hotel or rented facility, be honest about your expectations and your budget. It will save you both time and frustration in the long run.

Often, especially at larger facilities, there is a great deal of flexibility not only in the variety of food and beverages that can be offered, but in creative resources for giving your event that special pizzazz. If you don't see what you had in mind on the catering menu, ask to meet with the chef to customize a menu just for your event. Most chefs are delighted for the opportunity and unless you are preparing a rare dish, costs are generally not significantly more than ordering the banquet standard chicken breast.

At your initial meeting with a caterer, determine that the date is open on his or her calendar and then discuss the type of event you have in mind, the number of guests anticipated, the place you want to hold the event, any ideas on theme or special needs, the time of day, special colors for the linen to complement your decorations, and your approximate budget for catering services. Seek the caterer's creative input on food and its presentation, beverages, and decorations to develop your theme.

Because much of entertaining revolves around the serving of food, the quality, quantity, and presentation of that food are crucial. It is easy to fall into the trap of always using the same caterer and rerunning the same menus. Using the same caterer time and again, particularly when the same people are entertained repeatedly, can become boring.

Catering firms have personalities and special talents. One may be known for fantastic hors d'oeuvres, another may be expert at fabulous desserts, and yet another may excel at outdoor events such as barbecues or clambakes. Some specialize in theme events and arrive with the food, props, and costumed waiters to guarantee a fun time. Get to know the caterers in your area and trust word-of-mouth references. Cultivate relationships with a number of caterers so you won't be stuck if your favorite is too busy to handle an event for you or when the chef whose work you really love leaves for another job.

Try out a new catering firm on a smaller, less important event. Evaluate the quality of food, service, attitude and appearance of personnel, and the condition of the facility after they leave. Ask to look in on another function the firm is handling that is similar to the one you are planning.

• • •

The Menu

When selecting a menu, think of the people you have invited and the hour of the day. Will they have eaten dinner already, or will they be famished? Are there people in the group with religious or other dietary restrictions? Menus for luncheon should be lighter than menus for dinner, and menus for a predominately male group should be more substantial than menus for a group of women.

Don't overfeed people. Portions that are too large look wasteful, even unappetizing. If you offer a heavy luncheon in the middle of an all-day meeting, chances are that participants will be nodding in their seats by 2 p.m. By the same token, don't try to save money by sliding through the dinner hour with nothing more than hors d'oeuvres.

Offer the freshest seasonal foods your budget will allow, but don't make your selections so unusual that no one will eat them. If you are not sure what is in season, ask the caterer. Seafoods and fruits are examples of foods that can fluctuate wildly in price according to season. Americans today are very nutrition- and health-conscious. A high-fat, high-calorie menu will not be welcomed by many people.

If you are planning meals for a meeting lasting several days, look at the menus you have selected as a total package. Keep your selections and portions on the light side overall. People who will be sitting all day in meetings can become lethargic after they have spent several days consuming unfamiliar food and drink.

Never douse desserts or any other part of the meal with liqueurs or other alcoholic beverages. Many people object to the use of alcohol, and many take medications that could have dangerous reactions if alcohol were consumed. If you do serve liqueurs or alcohol-based sauces, present them in separate pitchers, clearly and attractively labeled.

If possible, have the caterer serve a test meal to you and several members of your committee. Although you may have to pay for this extra service, it is a wise investment. Use the opportunity to critique taste, presentation, portion size, and suitability for the occasion. This is also a good way to decide which wines best compliment the food.

• • •

Contracts: Get It in Writing

Once the menu is selected, you will seal the deal by signing a BEO (banquet event order), sometimes called an EO (event order). This is the contract that will serve as your event blueprint and the document from which everyone from the setup crew to the chef will take directions. Be sure to read it carefully, and don't leave anything to chance. Don't assume the caterers will know you want your break time a half-hour earlier than specified on the contract. If the BEO says a room should be set up theater style and you change to a classroom setup the day of the event, it will cost extra.

The BEO should contain every detail including start and end time, the names of every room to be used, break times, and complete setup instructions for each room.

If you have a complicated setup, ask for a diagram of the room.

Most contracts now call for a guarantee—that is, the number of people who will attend (or are expected to attend) the function—48 hours in advance. Typically, counts can be increased even on the day of the event but cannot be decreased once the guarantee deadline has passed. The guarantee is used to determine how many meals to fix, how many places to set, how many workers are required, and how much it all will cost you.

During preliminary planning discussions, you will estimate the number of people who will attend, and this is the number that will appear on your BEO. By the event date, this number could have gone up or down dramatically. Keep the caterer up-to-date on any significant change in your projected attendance, especially if special foods must be ordered.

When you give the guarantee, be conservative. The average no-show rate for any event is 10 percent, and the walk-in rate is very low. Never add to the guarantee; if anything, save money and reduce the number from what you actually expect. You will be billed for the number of guests you guarantee. If you originally estimated 150 people, and only 75 made reservations but you never called with a corrected guarantee, you will be billed for the original 150. It is standard for caterers to build a plus-or-minus 10 percent into this guarantee number. If you guarantee 100, but 100 show up, the caterer should have 10 extra meals ready. You will be billed for the full 100. If your counts exceeds the percent of overage agreed upon, the caterer is not responsible for supplying food for the unexpected guests, although most caterers will try to accommodate them.

Other points to check on the BEO are deposit, billing, and cancellation policies and the gratuity percentage that will be added to your bill.

How much food? How much money?

Food prices are typically quoted "plus plus"—meaning plus gratuity and plus sales tax, and generally the tax applies to both the food and the gratuity. Thus, for a luncheon priced at $12 per person, add the gratuity, usually at least 16 percent, to make $13.92. Then calculate the sales tax, 5 percent for example, on top of that figure to give the meal a cost of $14.62 per person.

Food costs may be quoted either per person (usually for a served menu) or per item (for a buffet). Per-item prices generally apply to expensive, unusual foods, such a fancy hors d'oeuvres, and can push counts up quickly. Don't make the mistake of thinking that a buffet will be cheaper than a sit-down meal. Buffet prices, especially for small groups, can be higher and are usually figured on one-and-one-half portions per person rather than the one serving per person you would pay if an item were served. Buffets for groups of less than 25 frequently carry a surcharge. Be wary of hors d'oeuvres buffets that are priced according to a number of pieces per person because portions are often skimpy and you are likely to run out of food. Do plan a mixture of hot and cold foods.

Find out when the caterers will need access to the facility, and notify the facility manager of your needs. Be aware that you will be billed for this extra time as well as for time needed for cleanup and removal of property and decorations following an event.

Ask what happens to leftovers. You will be paying for enough food for the number of people you guarantee, so leftovers are your property. Although many caterers are reluctant to agree to do so because they fear lawsuits, you can take leftovers with you after signing a release that absolves the caterer of responsibility if the food spoils because it sat in your car overnight. Because students are usually involved in special events at a university, you might offer them the leftovers. Or you can donate the food to a community shelter for the homeless.

Caterers may not volunteer to leave leftovers. In fact, often the only representatives of a catering company on site after an event are the cleanup crew, and they may not know their employer's policy on such matters. Get an agreement before the event, and be sure to clarify the policy on unopened items, such as beverages, that may be returnable.

One Saturday afternoon, as a guest at a pre-football luncheon, I was surprised to see the vegetable and dip tray left over from an event I hosted the previous evening. The tray had not been touched the night before, and because I had not requested that it be left, the caterers had returned it to the restaurant, which had recycled the tray and its contents.

• • •

Emergency Rations

Find out in advance what the caterer can supply quickly in the event that the food you ordered gets eaten too quickly and what it will cost. "Emergency" supplies of food can cost more than the original items. Also, remember that a hotel or conference facility with a kitchen provides much more flexibility in the event that you need extra food quickly. At a facility far from the caterer's kitchen, you may be out of luck.

Once we hosted a large group of alumni after a professional football game on a frigid November afternoon. An ample post-game hors d'oeuvre buffet had been planned, but people were so cold when they arrived that the first wave of guests ate all the hot food. Later-arriving guests were rightfully disgruntled, and the caterer could not provide backup food.

Knowing when to worry about backup food is an instinct that seems to develop with experience, and if you have done your planning carefully, this nightmare may never occur. Be prepared, however, and give one person the authority to order more food during the course of an event; identify that person to the catering manager. Instruct the catering staff not to bring out additional food or drink without the OK from that individual. Otherwise you may wind up with what happened at the post-game party: a bill loaded with $15 bags of potato chips as a result of our staff members telling the hotel waiters to provide bowls of snacks.

• • •

The Service Staff: From Black Ties to Blue Jeans

Discuss what uniforms the catering staff will wear. If the uniform style is inappropriate for your event, or if the color will clash with your decor, request another uniform. Most large caterers have several standard uniforms. A classic uniform suitable for a black-tie event is black pants or skirts with a white shirt and black bow tie.

If you have a generous budget or can build the expense into ticket prices, rent costumes to support your theme. The theater department may be a good resource. Some themes can be carried out with clothing people already own. A western theme, for example, is easy to interpret with blue jeans or jean skirts with western shirts. Enhance the outfits with bandannas and toy cowboy hats from the local discount store. Make string ties from a bolt of ribbon.

Regardless of what uniform waiters wear, good personal grooming is essential. Inspect the appearance of all wait staff before service begins. Long hair should be restrained, fingernails trimmed and clean, hands free from cuts or bandages, and clothing clean and pressed. Jewelry (if any) should be minimal and small enough that it will not drag in the food or catch on stemware.

• • •

Don't Forget the Dishes and Linen

Inspect the dishes, flatware, glasses, and serving utensils the caterer will use for your event. If they are shopworn, rent more presentable items from an independent supplier or have the caterer do this for you. When renting, stipulate who is responsible for transporting, cleaning, and returning the equipment; otherwise you could wind up with a kitchen full of dirty dishes and no one to wash them. If the facility you are using is equipped with china, glasses, flatware, and serving utensils, ask the caterer for consideration on the bill. Not having to transport such items saves the caterer substantial time and labor.

Tired serving dishes can be camouflaged by placing them in baskets or by arranging greens or cut flowers around their bases. Or you may be able to eliminate them entirely by using hollowed-out breads or vegetables like purple cabbage to hold foods like dips. Fruits, cheese, and hors d'oeuvres can be attractively displayed by piling them up in an arrangement like that in a still-life painting.

When your imagination conjures up a vision of tables dressed in linen reminiscent of Monet's garden, but your caterer's linen choices are limited to stained white or faded navy, it's time to call a linen rental company. Sprinkled in cities across the United States (check the yellow pages), linen rental companies offer an incredible array of tablecloths, napkins, skirting, runners, bows, and chair covers at reasonable prices. They have sizes and shapes that most campus catering offices don't (like cocktail-sized linen napkins) and specialty finishes (like metallic stripes). Hues include every shade on the color wheel, and patterned cloths run an intriguing gamut from romantic flowers to patriotic themes, sports and outer-space motifs, to classy white-on-white geometric designs. Rental companies ship virtually anywhere, and, after the event, you simply box the soiled linen and ship it back.

• • •

Something to Drink

Liability concerns, the prohibition of alcohol on many campuses, and the healthy-lifestyle craze have put cocktails on the endangered list at many campuses.

In the days when a cocktail party was standard for receptions and before dinner, deciding what to serve was simply a matter of locating the best liquor for the available budget and hiring a bartender.

Today, choosing drinks for this important social hour can be a challenge, but with planning and imagination, no one will miss the booze.

Ground rules: forget the old easy answers (serving soda pop is not allowed) and steer away from mocktails (drinks that are simply cocktails minus the alcohol). For cocktail lovers, mocktails are never as satisfying as the real thing and only remind them of what's not there.

Don't serve sticky-sweet punches based on ice cream or soda. Most adults don't care for the flavors, and they are too filling to serve before dinner. Instead, accentuate the positive. Work with your caterer to build a repertoire of light, sophisticated, nonalcoholic beverages that are pleasing to both the eye and palate and appropriate for many occasions. Include drinks that can stand alone for a reception as well as beverages with flavors and textures that compliment foods and can be served before dinner.

Try all concoctions before serving them at events, and cull the selections to include only those that taste good and look good, are not too sweet or heavy, and won't separate if left standing on a buffet.

Presentation is everything. Go for quality glassware whenever possible; not only is it environmentally friendly, glass is more pleasing to the eye and touch. For serving, round up a collection of vintage glass pitchers, easily found for very little money at secondhand stores or flea markets. Plan fresh fruit or flower garnishes to compliment each drink's color.

Fresh juices are refreshing and colorful. Try fresh orange or grapefruit juice mixed with a splash of seltzer. Serve in a balloon stem garnished with an orange twist or slice. Try blending fresh strawberries and bananas with crushed ice, garnished with a strawberry and a sprig of fresh mint.

Go exotic. Keep a supply of unusual bottled juices, such as pear, apricot, or grape in stock. To make a delicious grape spritzer, mix club soda, unsweetened grape juice, and lime slices. Serve in a fluted champagne stem with a slice of lime and a single fresh blossom.

Try designer water. Bottled, flavored waters, some carbonated, some plain, are a fun alternative to club soda. Inexpensive, not too sweet, and calorie-free, they are a delicious addition to any bar. Flavors commonly available include lime, lemon, cherry, black raspberry, and grapefruit.

Keep the sparkle. Sparkling cider and grape juice offer sophisticated taste and the look of bubbly champagne. Serve these as you would wines, about five ounces per person. Present in flutes to show off the bubbles.

Try tea. Hot, cold, spiced, or herb tea is a perennial favorite. For best flavor, serve properly brewed. (Never use instant.)

Think hot. When the weather turns chilly, work with your caterer to select a hot drink that is in keeping with the tone of your event. Classics such as savory bouillons, mulled cider, and spiced cranberry juice are satisfying appetizers.

Serve one choice only. Choose a beverage that compliments the food, and serve it, butler passed, as the only choice.

• • •

Serving Liquor

Caterers can supply wine and liquor, but they take a substantial markup. Typically, you will be charged a bartender fee and a setup fee on a per-drink basis. Your wine, poured by the catering personnel at the dinner table, will be assessed a per-person corkage or pouring fee. When planning a cocktail party, agree on what brands will be served. Unless you are having a very exclusive party or the honored guest has a known preference, avoid the more expensive "call brands." Make moderately priced selections, but avoid "brand X" liquors because regular drinkers can tell the difference. Never ask a hotel or restaurant if you can supply your own liquor. Not only is doing so an enormous legal liability for you, these businesses depend on food and beverage service, especially cocktails, for their profit margin.

Pricing policies vary—per drink, per bottle, or per person. No matter how it is calculated, expect to pay much more than if you bought the same bottle in the liquor store.

Make sure that bartenders pour drinks with a standard ounce-and-a-half jigger. If you are paying by the bottle, overpouring can drastically increase your costs. Ask that wines not be opened in large quantities or, when the event is over, you'll be stuck with opened bottles that were never poured.

Learn beforehand how leftover liquor will be handled. Empty bottles should be saved to verify the count. If you are paying by the bottle, opened bottles should be given to you, but you should not be charged for unopened ones.

Cocktails can be served from an open bar or cash bar. At an open bar, guests do not pay for their drinks, and the host picks up the tab for the entire party. At a cash bar, guests pay for their drinks as they order, either in cash or by purchasing tickets to exchange for drinks. A compromise between the two is to provide each guest with one complimentary ticket and sell additional tickets to those who want more.

Whichever option you choose, engage a professional bartender to pour the drinks. If students employed by your catering service will be pouring wine, passing champagne on a tray, or working at a bar, be certain they are old enough to serve alcohol legally.

Cocktail parties with an open bar can be very expensive. Control costs, and consumption, by setting a time for the bar to close and sticking to it. A pre-dinner cocktail party should last about 45 minutes; a half-hour is better.

Other cost-saving alternatives:

- a wine bar offering red and white wines,
- a wine punch, or
- theme drinks, such as hot toddies or bloody marys,

The dangers of alcohol

When I first started planning special events, alcohol was a prominent feature of most occasions. Hour-long cocktail parties often preceded a dinner that included white and red wines, a champagne toast, and an after-dinner liqueur. Needless to say, inebriated guests were common. Thankfully, today we are more aware of the dangers of too much alcohol. These days, planners are at great risk under social host liability laws (see Chapter 1).

Before planning an event that includes alcoholic beverages, make sure you clearly understand the policy of your administration and the laws of your state and municipality. In some states, it is illegal to consume alcohol on state or public property, to sell drinks or tickets for drinks without a liquor license, or to use state money to purchase alcoholic beverages. Federal funds provided through grant-funded programs often have similar restrictions.

The legal U.S. drinking age is 21. Therefore, avoid including students at an event where alcohol is served unless you are prepared to check identification and police the crowd.

Plan your function to reduce the chances of guests' drinking too much. Limit the length of cocktail parties and before-dinner receptions. Serve hearty hors d'oeuvres—carbohydrates, fats, and proteins. Fruits and vegetables are not enough. Salty snack foods such as nuts and chips will encourage your guests to drink more.

Coffee is a pleasant way to end an evening, but it does nothing to counter the effects of alcohol. Only time can do that. The body requires about one hour to burn off a typical drink—12 ounces of beer, five ounces of wine, or an ounce and a half of liquor. Stop serving all alcohol at least one hour before the event ends.

Finally, be prepared to deal with an intoxicated guest. Your bartenders should know how to cut someone off diplomatically. When and how to intervene is a difficult judgment call, but you owe all of your guests as pleasant an evening as possible.

As your guests prepare to leave, have a cab or a driver available so that a ride can be quickly and discreetly provided to any guest who should not be driving.

These suggestions are not just good manners; they are necessary to protect you from lawsuits. Many state and local laws hold the host responsible for the actions of an intoxicated guest. Make sure you know your legal obligations as a host, and act accordingly.

• • •

Over Budget? Here's Where to Cut

So you've planned the perfect party only to find that your tastes surpass your budget. How can you cut expenses without diminishing the quality of your event?

First, review the menu. Perhaps you can eliminate a course or switch to a less costly entree. Sometimes substituting different cuts of meat or reducing the portion size will do the trick. Consider eliminating the appetizer or expensive extras like shrimp, fancy cheeses, or exotic garnishes. On things like coffee breaks that have to be kept constantly full throughout a break period, request per person pricing. You will pay a set price per person rather than paying for the total amount provided, whether or not it is consumed. Here are some other tips.

- Share a menu with other parties being served that same day. You'll likely get a better price because preparing the same menu saves labor time in the kitchen.
- Explore changing from a buffet to a served meal. Consider eliminating dessert.
- A place to save big money is on the bar and wine service. Explore creative alternatives to an open bar. Unless toasts are planned, eliminate champagne. Consider whether wine is really needed with dinner.
- If entertainment is causing your budget to go into the red, eliminate it, limit the length of the performance, or search your campus for a quality student group. But never save money by hiring inferior entertainment.
- Decorations and flowers can also cause budget problems. Reduce the number and variety of flowers in the planned arrangement. Stay away from expensive flowers like roses and exotic tropicals that can cost several dollars per stem. Or do it yourself by ordering fresh flowers and greens and

arranging them in inexpensive vases or baskets.

- Eliminate such frills as custom-made favors, programs, menu cards, souvenir books, candles that require the purchase of holders and special chairs, or tables ordered just for one evening. Pare the guest list of university representatives who are "complimentary" guests but not really essential to the success of the event.
- Never trim the budget by reducing the quality of the food or drink or the number of service personnel.

• • •

Success Tips

Here are a few tips gleaned from years of front-line experience that should help you avoid or smooth over some common catering problems:

- Always order a few vegetarian plates as a backup in case some of your guests don't eat meat. When serving a seafood entree, order a meat entree backup in case someone is allergic to seafood. One such plate should be sufficient for a group of fewer than 50; if your group is larger, you may want to play it safe by ordering two or three. If these dinners aren't served, offer them to student workers. Many planners include a place on RSVP cards and meeting registration forms for the guest to note dietary restrictions.
- When hosting a VIP, call his or her secretary during the planning phase of your special event to find out favorite dishes and drinks as well as those to avoid.
- Always inspect the linen placed on the table for conspicuous patches and stains. Ask to have any that appear unacceptable replaced.
- Review the order and pace of service with the catering manager or captain before the function. Alert caterers to pauses for toasting. Give instructions about whether dessert plates should be taken up before the program begins and how long to continue serving coffee.
- Discuss the details of the table setting: sugar in packets or sugar bowls, butter pats on individual plates or a serving plate, salads and rolls preset or served.
- Request that cups and glasses be placed on the tables right side up instead of upside down as required in restaurants in many states.
- During a large event spread throughout a large facility, or when split-second cues are required, provide walkie-talkies to staff. Most hotel conference staff, engineers, and audiovisual technicians carry beepers. You can rent beepers for your key staff as well.
- Keep an emergency kit handy during the event with items such as a notepad; a corkscrew; a can opener; cash and a credit card; a master key and the keys to all cupboards, doors, and drawers; a cellular phone; and emergency phone numbers for campus security, the caterer, entertainers, bartenders, student workers, the florist, facility maintenance, and

audiovisual personnel. Also have extra placecards and the pen used to letter those already prepared; needle and thread; safety and straight pins; transparent and masking tape; a small hammer and screwdriver; first-aid supplies and aspirin; master copies of the order of events and guest list; projector bulbs and extension cords; business cards; and a spare pair of comfortable shoes.

• • •

When the Party's Over . . .

Clarify cleanup responsibilities. If you have rented a facility and engaged a caterer, you are obligated by the terms of your rental agreement. Be certain your caterer understands what is expected and readily fulfills any obligation to leave the facility in satisfactory condition and that all equipment and supplies be removed by the stipulated time. Otherwise, you will probably be charged for any extra cleanup required.

At the time a contract is signed and an event booked, many caterers require a deposit of between 20 and 50 percent of the total bill. Ask when the final payment is due. Some caterers will bill the client for the balance after an event; others want payment in full that day.

Be certain you understand the contract's cancellation clause. It will spell out exactly when you can cancel with no penalty or with a percentage penalty and when you must pay the entire amount. If you are planning a costly outdoor event and don't have a backup facility, you may want to purchase cancellation insurance to protect you from financial disaster in case you are rained out.

CHAPTER 5

Welcome

THE OLD SAYING "YOU ONLY GET ONE chance to make a first impression" is especially true for special events. How you meet and greet your guests will set the tone for the entire event, so get things off to a good start by welcoming them with warmth and efficiency. That means starting at the parking lot with welcome signs bearing the same name, colors, and graphic elements that you used in the invitations, announcement, and publicity. Next, get your name in lights by prominently displaying the event title on the hotel's outdoor lighted message board and interior function board.

• • •

Registration

A guest's next stop will likely be your well-staffed, organized registration desk. Position the registration desk prominently, but allow enough room so that guests waiting to register don't block the entrance to the room. When checking in a large group, divide people's names into logical categories, such as alphabetically or by class year, and mark the separate stations clearly, with overhead signs if possible. Have name badges and registration forms alphabetized and at the ready. Provide a table and chairs off to the side for guests who must fill in forms, pay, or write name badges.

A laptop computer can be an enormous help during registration, especially if there are questions about options a guest may have selected or money owed.

Plan to have adequate workers who have been briefed about how records are maintained, who has paid and who has not, and how to handle problems. If possible, have at least one floater at the registration table who deals with problems so that other guests are not delayed.

Most important, a senior event coordinator with authority to resolve all questions on the spot should always be available. Don't make a guest wait while a staff member tries to track down a person with the authority to make decisions.

The packet you give out at registration is an important public relations tool. Often your guests will have some extra time before the event starts and will thumb through your packet. Fill it with essentials such as tickets, parking permits, a campus map, a schedule with room numbers, and other pertinent documents, but also include some fun items like discount coupons for food or local attractions. It's also a good place to add your institution's entertainment and sports schedules, a keepsake such as a notepad and pen, and a sticker or decal.

Always include information about the facility you are using, including phone numbers for security, fire, and rescue. Provide information about hours and costs of services such as recreation; if possible, make arrangements to allow your guests to use campus facilities free of charge.

Move guests through the registration area quickly to keep traffic flowing. Position a well-stocked welcome table near the registration desk but out of the traffic stream where visitors can stop to pick up additional brochures or ask questions. Staff the table with friendly, well-informed people who are genuinely interested in making the guests feel welcome.

• • •

Welcoming VIPs

In some cases, it is appropriate and gracious to meet VIPs at the airport and escort them to campus or to arrange transportation for them. Be sure to communicate these arrangements clearly to avoid confusion. If you are welcoming dignitaries from other countries, research greeting customs beforehand to avoid making a blunder. VIPs frequently enjoy having a student among the escort party because it gives them the opportunity to gauge student opinion at the campus and provides insight for talks or speeches. But choose the escort carefully. As your institution's representative, he or she has a unique opportunity, perhaps one of the few quiet moments during the event, to talk to the VIP.

If your guest's accommodations are not close to the meeting facility, or if you are located in a city, it may be both gracious and expedient to provide transportation and assign an escort to the VIP to ensure that he or she doesn't get lost.

The question of who is paying for expenses should have been resolved, in writing, before the VIP's arrival. Double-check that appropriate arrangements have been made with the hotel, and verify not only with the sales office through which you may have booked the room, but also with the front desk, that payment instructions actually appear on the reservation. Doing so can help prevent an embarrassing and irritating experience later at the check-in desk. It's also a good idea to double-check other arrangements made for your guest such as car rental and the receipt of materials, like handouts, that may have been shipped to the meeting site.

It is a nice gesture to place a welcome gift in the rooms of speakers and VIP guests. A fruit or cheese basket, a bottle of mineral water or wine, flowers, or a small item embossed with the university seal is appropriate.

Those VIPs who do not require an airport welcoming committee should not have to wait in line at the registration table with everyone else. Instead, invite them to a private reception where you can welcome them appropriately and give them their name badges and other credentials.

• • •

Student Ambassadors

University students make excellent ambassadors of goodwill at special events. Recruit a corps of students to serve as hosts and hostesses for your organization throughout the year or on a per-event basis.

This group, as well as other staff and volunteers, should be fully briefed. Before each event, hold a meeting to familiarize everyone with the agenda, the reason for sponsoring the event, the location of all facilities, and general facts such as where to grab a quick bite to eat, where to buy university souvenir items, and the history and significance of campus landmarks.

Identify student ambassadors with armbands, lapel badges, ribbons, pins, or matching jackets or golf shirts. Assign some to specific duties, and station others in strategic places on campus to provide directions and answer questions.

• • •

Seating Arrangements

When the special event is a formal dinner or luncheon, seating arrangements can be a prime concern. Seating can facilitate important business relationships, foster friendships between key people who otherwise might not meet, and grease the wheels for crucial private support. At the same time, sparks can fly and all guests be made uncomfortable if seating arrangements are not planned carefully.

Seating for a special event requires more than a knowledge of the rules of etiquette. You need to know who's who on the guest list. Are there mortal enemies among them? Are ex-spouses going to be attending with new romantic interests? Is there someone your president needs to spend time talking with?

If you are not familiar with seating protocol, consult a good etiquette book. If you find yourself organizing an affair for elected officials or members of the military or diplomatic corps, be aware that there are specific rules for who is seated next to whom.

Of course, assigned seating requires placecards. These can be handwritten by someone with beautiful handwriting or done in calligraphy. Placecards should be positioned above the plate, propped against a glass, or left on top of the napkin. The lettering on the placecards should be large enough and there should be enough light at the tables so that guests do not have to bend over to read the cards.

Display a seating chart near the door of the dining room and assign staff members to help direct guests to their tables. (A seating chart, an alphabetical list of assignments, and a small flashlight are handy for this purpose.) Help guests remember their table numbers by giving them a small card with the table number written on it.

• • •

Open Seating

Open seating—guests can sit wherever they like—is used at informal occasions or where an advance guest list is not available. Try to keep all tables full to prevent gaps that make serving and conversation difficult. Varying the number of seats at tables can help. Mix seating for six, eight, and 10 people.

• • •

The Dais and Alternatives

The dais is one of the most frequently misused and misunderstood aspects of special event banqueting. The term literally means "throne of honor," but all too frequently, an odd collection of people gets stuck on the dais. The dais is reserved for honored guests only. With the exception of the spouse of the main speaker, spouses of the other dais guests are seated elsewhere. (In truth, the spouse of the main speaker would probably rather sit elsewhere, too.) Many event planners feel obligated to offer complimentary meals to dais guests, but it is perfectly acceptable to ask dais guests to pay for tickets, particularly at a fund-raiser. Just be sure to make this clear in the invitation.

I advocate eliminating the dais whenever possible at university functions. Because university entertaining frequently endeavors to mix outsiders with students, faculty, and staff, it is much more productive to place honored guests throughout the room so that more people have the benefit of talking with them. Students, in particular, are thrilled to rub elbows with a successful politician, businessperson, or celebrity, and the honored guest is spared the discomfort of being displayed on a platform.

As an alternative to the dais, try this: Place the podium on a small, low, easily accessible stage or riser with an attractive floral arrangement, national and state flags, or your institution's seal or banner. The guests who would normally be seated on the dais should be placed at tables close to the podium. A university representative can serve as host at each table. When it is time for the program, each person simply walks to the podium, speaks, and then returns to his or her table. This arrangement is particularly appropriate for award banquets involving many presenters and award winners who must walk to the podium, receive the award, shake hands, be photographed, and return to their tables.

For those occasions when a dais is absolutely essential, follow the rules for proper seating according to each person's role in the program. If the podium is located in the center of the dais, the host is seated to the right of it. Next to the host is the guest of honor. The second most honored guest is seated immediately to the left of the podium. On that person's left hand, the second host for the event is stationed. Host number three is seated between the most honored guest and honored guest number three, and so on, alternating back and forth between the right and left sides until all of the seats are filled. Try to have an even number of people on both sides of the podium, and never have anyone sit behind the lectern. Always have placecards on the dais, even when you don't use them for the rest of the guests.

The arrival and seating of dais guests is important to the successful orchestration of your event. If you have chosen dais guests properly, they are very special people and deserve to be a focal point. They should be treated with ceremony. To accomplish this, assemble dais guests in a private room beforehand. This gives them time to chat with university officials and other VIPs and enables you and the other hosts to welcome them individually. Brief them on the program schedule so they will be prepared when it is their turn to speak. Line up the participants in the proper order. When the rest of the guests are seated and quiet, either the maître d' or a designated staff member should announce them as they enter.

It is particularly effective if the band strikes up a march or does a drum roll or plays your alma mater if it isn't too slow and sweet. At this point, the audience should applaud as the honored guests file in, but you and your staff may need to start the applause.

When dais guests are seated and the room is quiet, the master of ceremonies takes over, first introducing himself or herself and then introducing each honored guest.

• • •

Mementos

Souvenirs are a nice extra touch and are fun to receive. Event favors can range from enameled lapel pins to a tiny box of chocolates stamped with your logo. There are many companies across the country specializing in souvenir items especially for the college market. You can personalize anything from plastic key rings to etched glassware to commemorate your event. When selecting souvenir items, try to choose something that is useful, tasteful, and somewhat relevant to the event. Check with event planners in other offices to see if you can order the same item for several functions (assuming there won't be much duplication of audiences) and divide the savings. Order well in advance.

• • •

Awards and Certificates

A traditional part of many special event ceremonies is the presentation of an award, trophy, certificate, or gift to the honored guest. In the past, silver trays, bowls, and loving cups were the traditional presentation items, but their expense and impracticality have greatly diminished their popularity. Today, presentation items are more likely to be beautifully framed certificates or photographs; crystal; or items made from polished wood and artificial materials.

All awards should bear the institution's full name and academic seal or motto and the date of presentation. Strive to make awards unique to your school, college, or university.

Formulate a master plan for awards, determine what items will be given for each presentation, and order a quantity of that item. For the most formal, prestigious recognitions, some institutions strike a medal with the academic seal on one side and the award name on the other. Hung on a neck ribbon of the institution's colors, medals make very attractive tokens and are perfect for the recipient to wear with academic regalia on future occasions. An attractive engraved certificate in a presentation folder should accompany each medal and should bear the recipient's name, the date, and the award name.

If a citation or proclamation is to be prepared for the honored guest, it should be written in calligraphy, embossed with the official university seal, and framed.

If the recognition item you have chosen is a plaque, select a model that can be engraved with the recipient's name.

Here are some additional planning tips:

- Order recognition items very early in the planning process. When ordering a quantity of items for a one-time event, always order at least two extras.
- Check engraving for correct spelling and dates.
- Don't give personal items such as clothing. When staff or coworkers have collected money to purchase a gift for an outgoing official, present the gift privately rather than at the podium during a banquet or ceremony.
- Remember to build the cost of recognition items into the special events budget.
- Practice the presentation ceremony, especially if an item such as an academic hood or medal must be placed over the recipient's head. Inform the recipient if he or she should be prepared to speak after the presentation.

CHAPTER 6

Raise the Curtain, Light the Lights

IT IS IRONIC THAT SOMETIMES THE PROGRAM content—the messages communicated from the podium—is almost lost in the flurry of planning details directed at making certain an event is perfect. Often, finalizing and fine-tuning the elements of the program are overlooked until the very last minute.

Selecting an emcee is one of a series of very important choices that should begin as soon as the event idea is born. At many universities, politics enter into the selection of an emcee, especially for a prestigious event. Typically, the alumni or development director, a vice president, a dean, or even the president wants to serve this role. A good criterion for choosing an emcee is to consider carefully the personality of the event and try to match it with the personality and talents of an individual. The emcee should be articulate, have a good speaking voice and a pleasant appearance, and be able to think on his or her feet. Often, there is someone on the event planning committee, or on your own staff, or who is otherwise involved with the institution who would play the part nicely.

Once the selection is made, meet with the emcee to review the order of events and to determine the cues for speakers, lighting changes, audiovisual presentations, music, and entertainment. Review the pronunciations of names. Meet with the emcee again immediately before the event to review plans or make changes, and give the person a script that notes everything he or she will need to know to keep the program on track.

• • •

Entertainment: Strike Up the Band

College and university campuses can provide great entertainment resources. Bright, talented students are usually available to provide everything from a variety show to piano or harp music during dinner. Using students showcases their talents and gives them the opportunity to perform in a real life scenario—and make a bit of extra money.

Music departments usually have a list of student and faculty performers who can add just the right touch to your event. Definitely audition talent before booking, and get to know the people who book student talent on your campus in order to get their advice and cooperation.

When hiring professional entertainers, follow up word-of-mouth recommendations, but audition the acts either by attending a performance elsewhere or by requesting a videotape. You will likely be working through an agent to arrange a booking. Always read contracts carefully, and get everything in writing. Professional entertainers often earn union-scale wages and are therefore considerably more expensive than student talent.

Entertainment should do more than just "entertain." It should help create the atmosphere you want and help break the ice between strangers by giving guests a conversation starter. Think creatively and explore widely—strolling musicians, mimes, craft demonstrations, a dance exhibition—the choices are limitless, so shop until you find whatever is appropriate for your event and budget.

Just before show time, review all aspects of the performance with the talent, such as when breaks will be and for how long, what type of music will be included, how loud it will be played, and when to conclude for the evening. Give the leader a script so he or she knows the big picture in terms of program content.

One note on dinner music: unless the performance is a concert, many of your guests will want to talk as the band plays, so make sure the music isn't too loud. While it's important to respect the band—if you didn't want them to play, you wouldn't have hired them—you also don't want your guests to have to shout as they try to carry on a pleasant chat.

• • •

Audiovisuals: Show and Tell!

Quality audiovisuals can greatly enhance your program. Messages sent through visual images have instant credibility and can help plant your message in peoples' minds. People remember things they see far longer than things they hear. Both seeing and hearing a message makes it even easier to remember.

Today's technology offers great versatility. In fact, technology is changing so quickly that presenters have a difficult time adapting their presentations rapidly enough to keep pace, and many facilities lack the necessary equipment.

Special effects using sophisticated audiovisual techniques can add a terrific kick to your special event program. One university wowed supporters with a demonstration of experimental computer technology at a fund-raising gala. The event's program relied on the projection of a computer-generated spaceship using new technology being developed in the university supercomputing center. In addition, special Internet lines created a live link between a man who lives on the other side of the world and guests in the auditorium. His image was projected into the hall as he was interviewed by the emcee.

One of the best special effects I ever saw was at a black-tie gala to launch a capital campaign. Late in the evening, after a lengthy program that included several speeches, the emcee introduced a video about life on campus. The room was dark, and the video rolled on, covering all phases of campus life and eventually turning to a football Saturday and the famed university band. Guests were jolted to their feet when the band marching on the screen became real, live band members marching into the ballroom. Their entry had been synchronized so that they appeared to march right out of the screen, playing the school fight song that had been in the video. Simultaneously, the house lights came up and the guests were on their feet clapping and singing. The room was instantly united and took on the feeling of a pep rally. As the fight song led into the alma mater, some guests were moved to tears.

At a prestigious private university, planners took audiovisual technology to a new level of daring when they created an outdoor show that told the university's history by projecting 40-foot-tall images of important university happenings and famous people onto the facades of historic buildings on the campus green. The computer-generated show used level-four lasers and four 9,000-watt projectors. The show required so much power that planners were concerned about causing a brownout in the city.

Rule number one when planning audiovisuals is do it right or not at all. Don't use poor audiovisuals or toss them into the mix as a gimmick. Programs need to fill a definite need and communicate specific information. Otherwise, it's not worth the time, effort, and often-considerable expense.

Many campuses have sophisticated media centers capable of producing a top-flight program. Students in photography, computing, film-making, or television production might also be willing to take on your project under the supervision of a professor. If you do not have such resources, or if you are pressed for time, enlist a professional agency. View samples and check references carefully. Set deadlines to keep the project moving forward and monitor progress regularly.

Don't get so fancy that you become a prisoner of your equipment. Instead, develop a product that has multiple uses and can be taken anywhere.

• • •

Sound Systems and Microphones

Few things are as annoying as a microphone or sound system that fails to function properly. Often the fault is not with the equipment but with the person trying to run it. For this reason, keep it simple. Use only quality equipment in good repair, even if you must go outside to rent it. Hotels have their own audiovisual equipment and the technicians to set it up.

Check out the sound in advance of every event by standing at the podium and speaking into the microphone while another person listens from different areas of the room. The old "testing one, two, three" is not an accurate indicator. Instead, read from the newspaper, raise and lower your voice, laugh, turn your head while talking, step back from the mike, lean down close to it. Have someone who is about the same height as the speaker stand before the mike and adjust it to the proper height.

Remember to turn the mike on before the program begins. Most speakers will assume that the microphone is ready and will be flustered if it is not. But turn it off during the meal to avoid broadcasting the head-table conversation to the audience.

If you are using recorded music or other recorded messages, be certain the recording is cued properly, and practice the cues before guests arrive.

• • •

Rehearse!

Music, sound, lights, audiovisual presentations, people entering and exiting the stage—you need a rehearsal to ensure things run smoothly. Arrange rehearsal time in the facility and include the techies, those critically important behind-the-scenes experts who control the lights, sound, and props. Because campus events often include people who have never before been behind a microphone or taken part in a production, it is a good idea to review every detail very carefully. Have people handle equipment like microphones exactly the way it will be done during the program. (Haven't we all experienced the ear-splitting electronic squeals caused when a speaker twists the mike around in a struggle to remove it from its stand?)

Rehearsal should include all parties (even if you have to pay them extra) involved in making the program run smoothly. Definitely rehearse processions to music so that the marchers get their pace down as well as entering and exiting the stage, stepping forward for a presentation, and even little details like the logistics of passing an award to a recipient's left hand so that he or she can shake hands with the right.

• • •

The Care and Feeding of Speakers

Whether you're hosting a small conference or arranging a national forum for debate, sooner or later you will be faced with identifying, contracting with, and caring for speakers.

On campus, speakers typically represent one of two groups: visiting faculty, government officials, and other experts who are willing to share their knowledge for little or no compensation; or big-name authors, celebrities, and professional speakers who command hefty fees.

You can help speakers give their best performances by attending to their basic needs and by making the trip to your campus as smooth and stress-free as possible. Here's how:

- Book early. Contact popular speakers, especially celebrities, at least a year in advance; six months is a minimum.
- Be specific. Tell the speaker why you want him or her and what you would like the speech to address. Mention the purpose of the event; the nature and size of the audience; how long the talk should be; who else and what else will be on the program; whether a meal is involved; and whether you

want the speaker to attend social events, mingle with students on campus, or meet with the press. Most experienced speakers have a repertoire of presentations that they tailor to audiences and will use your background information to determine if their material matches your needs. Most won't be willing to prepare a presentation or speech from scratch.

- Don't be shy. Discuss fees, perks, and expense reimbursements up front. If you are booking a celebrity or professional speaker, this will be done with the speaker's agent or a speakers bureau.
- Get it in writing. As soon as an oral deal is reached, follow up in writing. Ask the speaker to sign and return a copy of the agreement—even when you are working with unpaid volunteers.
- Work ahead of deadlines. Don't wait until the last minute to request biographical information, photos, and written descriptions of workshops or speeches.
- Never title a presentation. Don't name a speech, describe its content, or publish biographical information without the approval of the speaker.
- Be sure. Fax a copy of your promotional piece to each speaker for approval before it is published. Set a deadline for reply. This is particularly important for workshop and conference speakers whose presentations are to be capsulized in promotional brochures.
- Stay in touch. Establish a dialog with the speaker or his or her office personnel between the time of agreement and the speaking date. Send copies of promotional materials.
- Make travel arrangements early. Be certain the speaker knows whether you will make the arrangements or if he or she should. Be clear about who will initially pay for travel. Will the speaker pay first and file for reimbursement, or will you make and pay for arrangements? Before booking, find out speakers' airline preferences. Many large cities have more than one airport; ask which is most convenient. Find out about preferences for in-flight meals such as vegetarian dinners or fruit plates. Try to avoid scheduling a speaker's arrival on the day of the speech—the likelihood of off-schedule flights due to weather or other problems is too high.
- Book and confirm quality accommodations. Find out if your guest wants a smoking or non-smoking room. Put a hospitality gift in the room such as a fruit and mineral water basket, fresh bread and cheese, candies, or flowers. Speakers appreciate information about the university and, in the case of a conference or meeting, a copy of the agenda, roster of participants, and locations of meeting rooms. Leave the local phone number of a contact person in case the speaker has questions or problems.
- Be sure the room is in good repair and away from noisy areas of the hotel such as the swimming pool or cocktail lounge.
- If the speaker will stay in university accommodations, provide specific directions about location and check-in. Alert university personnel to expect your special guests. Avoid accommodating speakers in private homes.

- Assign an escort. Strange cities and unfamiliar campuses can be confusing. The last thing a speaker needs is to get lost or to struggle to find parking or the correct campus building. Speakers should be escorted door-to-door by a student or staff member who has access to VIP parking areas. If the speaker is flying in, pick her up at the airport, transport her throughout the visit, and plan to drive her back to the airport.
- If the speaker is traveling by car, give good directions in writing, and provide a map of your area. Include the hotel's full street address and phone number.
- The day of the talk, send an escort to lead the speaker to the meeting room.
- Allow some quiet time. Don't exhaust your speaker by overscheduling. Most speakers need rest to be at their best, and most want time alone for about an hour before the talk to concentrate, review notes, and freshen up. Don't surprise your speaker by adding last-minute functions to the agenda.
- Arrange a proper introduction. The person introducing the speaker should have accurate information and properly pronounce the speaker's name. It's a good idea to rehearse the introduction.
- Watch the time. Keep the program on schedule, and don't rearrange the order of speakers unless it is an emergency.
- Hire someone to run audiovisual equipment. It is well worth having paid audiovisual staff on site to adjust microphones, operate slide projectors, cue videos, and troubleshoot possible problems.
- Provide each speaker with fresh water at the podium.
- Check the podium. Be sure it has a paper rest to secure notes and a working light to enable the speaker to read in a dimly lit hall or during audiovisual presentations.
- Check it again. Make sure that all wires are secured to the floor, that legs of easels are snapped firmly in place, that flip charts are attached to easels, that markers are fresh and functioning, and that audience views are not obstructed by audiovisual equipment. Keep awards to be presented, large floral arrangements, other speakers' audiovisual equipment, and other distractions away from the podium.
- Get good photos. If the media will be present during the talk, hang your university banner behind the podium so that it appears in photos and on TV.
- Arrange lighting so that the speaker can be seen even when slides or videos are being shown. Otherwise, your star becomes a faceless voice in the darkness.
- Tell the speaker how to dress. Will audience members be in black tie, in business attire, or just in from the golf course?
- Will there be questions? Decide beforehand whether the speaker will answer questions and for what period of time. Have a moderator ready to cut off questions promptly at the time limit.

- Have the check ready. Hand the speaker the honorarium in an envelope just before he or she departs. If you are working with an agent, mail the check to the agent the same day; she will pay the speaker. If your speaker is unpaid, immediately send a letter of thanks.
- Reimburse promptly. Mail travel reimbursement forms to the speaker's office no later than the next day.
- Tell them how they did. If participants evaluated workshop speakers, give the presenters the results, even if they are not particularly good. Speakers especially appreciate comments and suggestions and use them to perfect future presentations.
- Send a thank-you note and copies of press clippings.

• • •

Contractual Obligations

No matter how you book a speaker, you will need a contract. An agent or speakers bureau will provide a contract. If you are making your own arrangements, you will need to draw up the contract.

A contract should specify all this:

- The speaker's compensation and how and when it will be paid. Standard terms are usually 50 percent to be paid at booking, 50 percent after the engagement.
- Performance requirements. This is a clause that describes the agreed-upon general content and states whether the information will be tailored to your group and whether the speaker will be required to research your group beforehand through surveys or interviews. It can include prohibitions against such things as the use of vulgar language. The clause needs to specify how satisfaction will be measured, usually by written audience evaluations. It is becoming common for as much as 25 percent of the fee to be tied to performance. It is a good idea to state in the contract that the speaker is solely responsible for content and that your school does not necessarily endorse the speaker's point of view. Such a statement may also help protect you in case the speaker is sued for unauthorized use of someone else's material.
- Who is responsible for duplicating handouts. It's smart to specify a deadline and maximum length. The same applies to overheads and slides.
- Who is handling travel arrangements and accommodations. If you will be paying the speaker's expenses, specify how receipts are to be submitted and by what deadline. Watch out for extras like first-class airfare and luxury items such as brands of bottled water, specifications for fresh flowers in the dressing room and similar luxury add-ons. Strike these from the contract to help keep expenses down.
- Responsibility for staging, sound systems, and props. Many speakers prefer certain brands and arrangements of sound systems or complicated

audiovisual setups. Before signing, double-check how much it will cost to rent, move, install, and run such equipment. Be sure the facility you have chosen can accommodate it. Find out in advance if you will need to hire technicians and how much it will cost.

- If the speaker will meet with students or appear at press conferences, receptions, or autograph sessions. If a rehearsal is required, the time and place should be stated.
- How the contract can be terminated without liability. Typically this clause includes acts of God or illness of the speaker. In either of these cases, the speaker must return deposits paid by your institution.

• • •

Ways That Might Save Money

Offer to let your speaker sell her books, tapes, and other merchandise before or after the talk. A book signing arranged in cooperation with the university bookstore can work well and may generate some media coverage.

Some speakers will reduce or even waive their fees for nonprofit organizations. If your purpose and the speaker's cause are closely matched, do your homework to put together an incentive package that helps you both achieve goals. Be flexible on the date. If the speaker will be in your city or area on other business, you may be able to piggyback on the date and get the person you want at a bargain price.

• • •

Stay Out of Trouble

The ideas and materials used during a speech are the property of the speaker. You may not record or copy these without written permission. If a speaker agrees to let your organization sell tapes or other materials, typically he or she will earn a percentage of each sale. Get all such agreements in writing.

CHAPTER 7

Work With Volunteers

THE ROLE OF VOLUNTEERS IN SPECIAL events planning varies tremendously from campus to campus. Some campuses use them for every event, while others rarely involve them. Some colleges have standing committees, while others form committees as needed. At every institution, there are times when involving volunteers is good public relations and essential to accomplishing all that needs to be done. Such occasions include an anniversary, a capital campaign, or a once-a-year gala. If your special events staff is small, volunteers can be invaluable.

The prospect of working with volunteers, however, makes many special events planners cringe. Volunteers and the committees they form have a way of slowing the planning process, confusing issues and purposes, disregarding budgets, and in general making work for planners. The event planner's cry of frustration is "I could do this so much more easily myself!" However, the fact is that volunteers are an integral component of success.

Large events often use several hundred volunteers working in every imaginable capacity from committee chairs to greeters. There is a good reason for this many people: volunteers are frequently expected to buy tickets, to purchase tables, to bid for auction items, and to recruit others to do the same. The larger and more visible the committee, the quicker new people are to jump on the bandwagon, bringing new money along with them. This is particularly true when committee members are socially prominent VIPs, media or sports celebrities, or corporate CEOs. The volunteer structure and the excitement and visibility it creates become an important part of event publicity and a powerful marketing tool. Volunteers are the recruiters, ambassadors, and sales representatives for the event.

The volunteer structure needed for a large-scale fund-raising event may surpass any you have previously worked with. But as daunting as a massive volunteer system sounds, large events are impossible to do alone. A well-organized, well-managed system can save you work and preserve your sanity.

• • •

Volunteers Have Much to Offer

Volunteers are the link between the visions of administration and faculty and the external people who have the wherewithal to make visions realities. Volunteers can give you access to social circles, to the corporate community, to politicians, and to community resources. As outsiders willing to commit time, energy, and money, volunteers add a measure of credibility to your cause. By sharing in the planning and implementation of your event, volunteers develop a sense of ownership and become committed to its success with a pride and enthusiasm that are contagious.

Volunteers can give you a fresh perspective, new ideas, and insights into the inner workings of your target audience. The secret to success in working with volunteers lies in developing mutual respect and in learning how to channel everyone's energies toward reaching goals.

• • •

Volunteers Have Changed

Today's volunteers are much different from the volunteers of years past. Now, planners often find volunteer rosters filled with skilled professionals who are experts in their own fields and can offer experience and knowledge that sometimes exceed that of the planner. Many corporations lend their executives to nonprofit organizations (especially for fund-raising events) as part of good corporate citizenship. This is particularly common when corporations have underwritten an event because it helps ensure sponsor input as well as an element of quality control.

In a university setting, planners can frequently enjoy the volunteer input of retired faculty and staff—a real boon to attracting support because many alumni have deep affection for and loyalty to faculty, and, after long careers, faculty and staff know many people.

The changing face of volunteers challenges planners to upgrade their own skills. These range from the productive management of meetings to the honing of the diplomatic skills necessary when dealing with people used to being in charge.

At a conference of alumni and development professionals, participants produced a list of 35 reasons people volunteer their free time. Among the reasons:

- belief in the organization,
- desire to help the institution achieve its goals,
- a way to meet new people and get involved with the community,
- career advancement,
- a creative outlet for talents and skills,
- desire for self-fulfillment by helping others,
- desire to be recognized as an active community leader,
- desire to be recognized for a job well done, and
- because a friend asked them to get involved.

These are many of the same reasons that donors contribute dollars and that staff members choose to hold their positions. In other words, volunteers and staff members share similar beliefs and motivations for wanting events to be successful. Why then do dissatisfaction and frustration frequently enter the picture for both parties? And how can you prevent it from happening on your campus?

• • •

Communicate Goals Clearly

A major source of problems between staff members and volunteers can be a lack of communication of goals. As a full-time staff member immersed in day-to-day operations, you may sometimes forget that not everyone knows the same range of details about the institution that you do. Volunteers may envision your campus the way it was in their student days 20 years earlier. They may be unaware of the budget cutbacks that you take for granted as a fact of daily life; they may know nothing of important changes in administrative structure and leadership.

Long before any volunteers are recruited, goals and objectives for events should be set by the administration and the appropriate boards. Once these goals are endorsed and presented to the staff, it becomes the staff responsibility to relay them to volunteers.

• • •

Who's in Charge?

It is important for key volunteers and staff members to understand the lines of authority and responsibility. Before committees are fleshed out, key volunteers and staff liaisons should meet with top administrators to reach an understanding and to hear goals articulated and boundaries drawn.

During the event planning process, one person should be in charge of making final decisions regarding expenditures and approval of committee ideas. Especially when events involve hundreds of people and many thousands of dollars, it is imperative that boss, staff members, and volunteer leaders be clear on who reports to whom, who mediates disputes, and who casts the decision-making vote.

• • •

Recruit Doers

Because the main goals of special events are to make friends and raise money, recruit those volunteers who will make contributions and lead you to new donors without requiring you to invest a lot of time and money in education and cultivation. In other words, when recruiting, tap directly into people who are already interested in the area to be promoted or funded and probably have a network of friends who share their views.

The success of the event will be in direct proportion to the quality and commitment of the people recruited to serve as volunteers. Solid volunteer and committee structure become paramount when selling tickets, securing underwriting, finding unique auction items, and negotiating for services at bargain prices. It could mean the difference between a successful event and one that is poorly attended or doesn't raise money.

Top volunteers should be people of action who can be relied upon to follow through on commitments. Committee chairs should be prominent members of your target audience who can talk to other influential people on a peer level.

Look for volunteers who have the personality and social standing to persuade others to support you and to attract members of your target audience, and who have the charm and grace to make everyone feel welcome and needed.

One frequently overlooked resource is people who are members of friends groups because they have contributed to a particular cause. Friends groups are commonly found for art, music, the library, and athletics, although many institutions have friends groups for such diverse areas as journalism and hotel and restaurant management. Unfortunately, even though these individuals have made the most tangible demonstration of interest, they are frequently the last ones called upon to help plan and promote events.

Another good hunting ground is the roster of persons who register for continuing education courses. This is a particularly good way to identify community members who may not have any other affiliation with your campus, but who may have interest in specific areas. One smart director of a school of art discovered the name of the wife of a prominent local banker on the roster of a continuing education art course. He asked her to serve as a volunteer for his newly formed friends group. Even though the woman had had little contact with the university, she quickly became an exemplary volunteer and a major donor, drew her husband's influential friends and business contacts into involvement, and ultimately created an endowment that helped build a new wing on the art building.

The alumni association is an excellent source of volunteers. Alumni staff members have vast networks of alumni acquaintances and can provide background information about an individual's areas of expertise, interest, previous volunteer experiences, and giving potential. This is a particularly good resource when you are planning an event that will take place in another city or during a capital campaign when events may be staged in many different locales. Don't overlook existing alumni chapters as a ready source of reliable, motivated volunteers.

Make the adage "if you want something done, ask a busy person to do it" work for you. Read local and regional society pages to learn who volunteers for what causes and which corporations get involved. These people and corporations may be willing to help your cause, too. Scan the published lists of patrons of benefits put on by other organizations to help match names you recognize and their interests with your volunteer needs.

Once you have recruited the top volunteer leadership, ask each person to recruit his or her own subcommittee members and volunteer workers. In this way, you can take advantage of the power of friend asking friend, which will encourage a degree of commitment and camaraderie. A word of caution, however: Active, vibrant volunteer structures must have a constant influx of new, enthusiastic people.

While relying on top volunteers to recruit their friends is a bonus, guard against the impression that your volunteer network is a clique that not everyone can join. Communicate this philosophy to volunteer leaders, and get them committed to encouraging a continual infusion of new blood.

Reach out to volunteer prospects by inviting them to an open house to explain your purposes and to ask them to join a committee. Publicize organizational and recruiting meetings through the local press, campus newspaper, and alumni publication, using free space such as community-calendar columns as much as possible. During your main recruiting push, buy advertising space in publications that are most likely to be read by your potential volunteers. If you have a yard sign at your building or a bulletin board in a well-traveled area, post meeting particulars and stress that everyone is welcome. Post the same message on your Internet site.

When you need a large number of volunteers quickly, plan a volunteer recruitment party and have each volunteer bring a new person. Try a friendly competition and reward volunteers for recruiting new people through incentives such as free tickets to campus plays or shows, university souvenir items, or passes to athletic events. Recognize all volunteers for their efforts. A small, inexpensive gift such as a leather bookmark embossed in gold with the university seal is always a good motivator.

Use the talents of veteran volunteers and give them a meaningful role in recruiting by asking them to identify what types of skills are needed to flesh out volunteer ranks. Next, have veterans lead recruitment meetings and work as hosts and hostesses to make newcomers feel welcome and to answer questions. Ask new volunteers to complete an information sheet that includes name, address, phone numbers, employer, and areas of interests or special skills, like calligraphy. Collect the sheets at the end of the meeting because many people will listen to the entire program before deciding whether to sign on. Distribute a brief fact sheet about your volunteer program, and include the name and phone number of a staff person who can answer questions and provide more information.

• • •

Form Committees

Well-organized, properly managed committees are the most efficient, creative way to bring events into successful reality. A committee that has a variety of members with different skills, backgrounds, and points of view ensures the greatest flow of creative ideas and spreads the burden of work among many.

Committees can also save you time because details can be worked out in meetings instead of tying up your time or that of the entire group of volunteers or of the executive committee. However many committees are involved, try to match the interests and abilities of the committee chair and the members with the tasks to be completed. Then step back and let the committees run their own affairs, generating ideas and making decisions without your constant input and supervision.

Sometimes it makes sense to use only one committee, while at other times you'll need a complex committee structure. When deciding which arrangement best fits your needs, focus on your goals in public relations and fund-raising, and remember that volunteers should be used for their talents and abilities to advance your cause, not as a source of free labor.

Here are several typical volunteer structures.

A standing committee

An easy, efficient way to organize volunteers for an academic year, a celebration year such as an anniversary, or a fund drive or capital campaign is to form a central events planning committee. This becomes the group from which all planning originates and from which all other committees derive. The committee works with college staff to coordinate all events, including both friend-raising and fund-raising, for a given span of time.

When forming the committee, select people for their leadership, experience, willingness to work hard, ability to attract support, and skills in motivating others. Establish officers within the committee and move people through the chairs on an annual basis. This guarantees continuity and gives you a method to gracefully phase out old volunteers and bring new ones on board.

Customize your overall committee structure from this point to suit your needs by assigning people to chair specific events and by adding subcommittees.

A volunteer is in charge

Traditionally, fund-raising events are chaired by a top volunteer. He or she forms an executive committee responsible for shaping the event by making major decisions about its scope and tone as well as for ensuring that it achieves its fund-raising goals. A college or university staff member serves as liaison to this committee. The chair can generate numerous subcommittees responsible for attending to details such as decorations, invitations, ticket sales, food, and entertainment. Members of the executive committee chair the subcommittees. Thus the volunteer structure forms a pyramid that continues to grow broader at the base as new volunteers are recruited throughout the planning stages.

Before this army of volunteers begins its work, the college or university executive and the event chair agree on goals for the event, both in terms of public relations and, if it's a fund-raiser, the dollars to be raised. They establish the general framework and a chain of command. The executive committee takes over and proceeds with minimal staff input.

While this system leaves staff members free to attend to other duties instead of spending countless hours in committee meetings, such an autonomous committee may not always make the decisions you want, and countermanding their decisions can be very sticky. This structure is useful, however, when you are working with a small professional staff with many other duties or when there are many events on the schedule, such as during a celebration year or capital campaign. A carefully trained, reliable group of volunteers who can be counted on implicitly is essential for success. A bonus of this arrangement is that volunteers are free to brainstorm and implement their own ideas—something that most people thrive on.

If you choose this structure, you will need to establish reporting and coordinating mechanisms between yourself and the committee. This coordination will help your volunteers avoid stepping on toes and approaching prospects who may be already targeted for other projects and will also ensure that proper gift-acknowledgment procedures are followed.

You are the event chair

Many college and universities want a professional staff member to chair the standing event committee or the executive committee for a specific event. The staff member forms an executive committee of top volunteers, each of whom chairs a subcommittee and becomes responsible for recruiting his or her workers. A variation of this plan occurs when a professional staff member is assigned to manage the committee as a co-chair with a volunteer. When the staff member chairs a specific event committee, he or she assumes the responsibilities of the volunteer chair described above.

Assigning committee control to a staff member means that more decision-making authority remains in-house. Also, the staff member becomes a clearinghouse for information and the common link that increases efficiency and helps to guarantee consistency for all of the year's events. When a staff member chairs a standing events committee, less time is wasted in reinventing the wheel for each event, and some resources can be allocated more efficiently. For example, a staff member can negotiate a better price for food by offering the caterer several jobs instead of one and can establish solid relationships with suppliers. It is also easier to track donor records and to avoid asking the same people repeatedly to make donations or to purchase tickets.

Unless the staff member is a skillful manager, however, volunteers may feel that this arrangement decreases their opportunities for creative input. They are likely to feel less committed to getting tasks completed and attending committee meetings because they know that responsibility ultimately rests with the paid staff member.

• • •

Train and Motivate

Recruiting good volunteers is only the beginning. Once you have signed up the volunteers, you need to involve them in a productive, meaningful way that is satisfying to them and beneficial to you.

First, be certain that everyone who volunteers is contacted immediately. Even if the planning for the event will not begin for months, you should send all volunteers a note thanking them for volunteering and giving them an idea of what will happen next and when. It is discouraging when a person volunteers but doesn't hear a word for months or is never called on at all. Neglect opens the door for people to grumble to their associates about you and your lack of organization.

As you organize the executive committee and subcommittee structures, carefully match volunteer interest and skills with the jobs to be done. Strive to make the most of your volunteers' time by assigning them to tasks they can do and enjoy doing. Every volunteer knows that sooner or later there will be unglamorous jobs like stuffing envelopes, but they will do these more cheerfully if the major portion of their position is meaningful.

If, after reviewing the job description, a person decides that a position is more than he or she can manage, it is better to learn this before planning begins than to have catastrophe strike later. Job descriptions for subcommittee members can be given orally in a training session by the subcommittee chair or the executive committee member in charge of the particular event.

All volunteers deserve the same respect you would give a paid worker, including the right to know what you expect of them and when. Prospective executive committee members should see a written job description before they accept the position. This step protects them as well as you. A job description formalizes the activity, communicates the seriousness of the responsibility, and helps the person make an honest assessment of the time commitment.

If yours is a fund-raising event, let executive committee members and the event chair know early on that they will be expected to purchase tickets, preferably at the highest level. The reasons for this are twofold. First, the event budget cannot accommodate more than a few complimentary tickets and remain within budget or reach fund-raising goals. Second, top volunteers are usually people of means who have friends in influential positions. By purchasing patron-level tickets or buying an entire table at a gala, the volunteer sets the pace for his or her friends and associates and is in a stronger position to ask them to participate at the same level.

When organizing fund-raising event volunteers, inform them that volunteers will not receive complimentary tickets. Clearly communicate that this is because the purpose of the project is to raise money for the cause, not just to have an event. If all your volunteers attend the event for free, you would probably not meet the fund-raising goal.

At training sessions for all volunteers, explain the project and its goals and objectives in the same manner that you used to train executive committee members. Include features to bring the project to life such as tours, talks from key people, or sneak previews of construction blueprints. Strive to create a link between volunteers and the project in order to build their understanding and support.

As the planning process moves from the idea phase to the implementation phase, you may need to hold another training session.

Establish a mentoring system that pairs new volunteers with veterans during initial phases of event planning and during ticket sales. This makes veterans feel needed and gives newcomers more confidence, helps ensure quality control, and saves you from answering the same questions over and over.

• • •

Make Meetings Count

Effective committee meetings begin on time, end on time, and don't waste time in the middle. Every meeting should have a clear purpose that can be stated in a few sentences and a written agenda that is distributed to every member beforehand.

Meetings should be confined to one hour—less whenever possible. Efficiency and time limits are imperative; most volunteers have busy schedules and cannot spend hours in marathon discussions that produce little. Committee chairs should be well versed in meeting management and know how to limit circuitous discussion and keep the meeting on track. Keep minutes for each meeting, and distribute them to committee members to prevent confusion about what decisions were reached and who is responsible for what. Before each meeting ends, the chair should make clear assignments and note them in the minutes.

One way to keep committee meetings to a reasonable length and to help guarantee attendance is to hold them at lunchtime in a convenient location. Invite members to bring a brown-bag lunch or offer sandwiches, but don't go to a restaurant; it's hard to accomplish anything in this setting. If you are working with an executive on loan, try meeting at that person's office or hold the meeting right after work in a location that most members can get to easily on the way home. This prevents people from going home and getting too relaxed or too involved in other things to leave the house again. And committee members with small children won't need to find a babysitter for the evening.

The two greatest detriments to successful committee work are rambling sessions that seem to last forever without producing significant decisions and meetings that seem to exist only for the sake of meeting. Committee members are sending clues that meetings are nonproductive when they leave early or don't show up at all. If you keep the meetings short and to the point, with an action agenda and clear assignments, members will attend because they know their time will be spent productively.

• • •

Give Volunteers Room to Work

Volunteers need a dedicated work space where they can spread out projects on tables, maintain files, use the telephone, and close the door when they need privacy. Resist the temptation to furnish the volunteer office with rejected furniture and an outdated computer. Instead, make the dollar commitment to provide a modest but up-to-date work environment stocked with basic office supplies and equipment that works. A computer and printer loaded with software that is compatible with yours are essential. Add a large bulletin board or a write-on, wipe-off wall calendar to post notices about upcoming committee meetings, important dates, and assignments.

Keep a computer file or a reference notebook of all volunteers, whether currently active or not, with name, address, telephone numbers, and pertinent information about skills and interests for everyone who has offered to help.

Minimize requests to office staff by training volunteers in office basics such as where to find supplies, how to run the photocopier, how to fill out standard forms, how to place long-distance telephone calls, how to schedule the conference room, and how to operate the office coffeemaker.

Conversely, inform the office staff about the important role volunteers play in your success and tell them about the privileges volunteers have been given regarding use of office equipment and supplies. Teach staff how to work diplomatically with volunteers and where to turn if there is a conflict.

Whenever possible, designate one clerical staff member to work regularly with volunteers. On large projects such as a campaign that may entail planning many events, sending hundreds of invitations, processing checks, and keeping accurate records, hire temporary secretarial support for the volunteer office.

By dedicating a professional work space for volunteers, you convey the message that you respect them, that their projects are serious business, and that their work is important. In return, a well-organized work space will greatly increase volunteer efficiency and output. After all, volunteers are there to help you get the work done, not to create more work for you and other staff members.

• • •

Staff and Volunteer Relations

Sometimes, staff may show turf-guarding behavior and feelings of resentment toward volunteers. This may be particularly true for those staff members who are not part of the decision-making process. Resentment can build when staff members feel that volunteers can do anything they want and that all volunteer ideas are accepted and acted upon regardless of previous office policies and when staff people feel a threat to their own job security.

On the other hand, volunteers often feel like second-class citizens who have not been told everything they need to know to get the job done and who walk the uncomfortable line between needing to be in an office regularly but not being on the "real" staff.

Friction between staff and volunteers can build quickly if staff members feel that volunteers get all of the "fun" assignments. When the excitement, glamour, and frenetic pace of events planning begins to emanate from the volunteer office but the routine of regular duties continues for everyone else, tempers can flare and cooperation crunch to a halt. Feelings are manifested through seemingly trivial complaining; staff members grumble that volunteers are too noisy, and volunteers complain that they can't get a turn to use the photocopier.

It is easier to prevent this situation from developing than to resolve problems as they happen. Start out by clearly delineating the roles of staff and volunteers and assuring each group of its importance to the long-term success of the institution.

Forge a bond between the two groups by focusing on goals to be achieved and the need to pull together as a team. Personalize the relationship by helping people get to know one another as coworkers. An easy way to do this is by inviting volunteers to join staff over pizza at lunchtime, by introducing volunteers so that people know one another by name, and by treating each group with an equal standard of professional respect. The beginning of the academic year or the beginning of a major fund drive or campaign should always include a time for volunteers to gather and get acquainted with one another and with the staff.

• • •

Recognition and Rewards

Volunteers thrive on frequent recognition and rewards. There is no more effective way to keep volunteers happy and productive than through positive feedback. Many people wait until an event is completed or a committee's term is fulfilled to give recognition.

Instead, keep motivation high by giving recognition often in the form of praise to the group, frequent handwritten notes, and telling volunteers how much you appreciate their efforts.

At the event, display the names of all volunteers on an attractive poster and print them in the program.

When the event is over, present everyone who helped with a small token reminiscent of the event or a souvenir item from your college or university. Give executive committee members a more substantial gift, and present something extra-special to the event chair. If your budget permits, host a recognition tea or other gathering with volunteers, college or university officials, and, if yours was a fund-raising event, the recipients of the proceeds.

CHAPTER 8

Budget for Success

BUDGETING FOR SPECIAL EVENTS IS always part guess and part gamble. Events grow and change between concept and implementation, prices of food fluctuate, and the guest list can balloon at the last minute. There never seems to be enough money to do everything you would like to do. Nevertheless, you need to build a budget and stick to it. When an event is intended to make money, this task becomes paramount.

Step one is to build a budget based on facts. Once you have determined the type and scope of your event, gather actual costs from all suppliers. Don't forget to include expensive but hidden costs such as liability insurance, overtime for workers, and transportation for guests, if needed.

If you are having an event that will be paid for out of university resources, determine whether the projected costs are affordable and scale plans downward if necessary. If you are contemplating a money-making event, your budget planning work has just begun.

• • •

How Much Needs To Be Raised?

The extra step in budgeting for fund-raising events is knowing how much money you need to raise and factoring this amount into the overall budgeting formula. This, in turn, determines the number of tickets you need to sell, the sponsors you need to find, and how much you must charge.

You should have a firm fund-raising goal before event planning begins. In fact, the type, scope, and focus of the event will be shaped in large part by this number. Once the fund-raising goal is set, follow these steps to figure out how much you will need to cover all expenses and meet the goal.

1. Select a type of event that will best appeal to your target audience.
2. Research the costs of this event.
3. Add the fund-raising goal to the event costs.

Now is the time for pragmatic decision making. Consider the total: Is it realistic to attempt to reach it with the kind of event you have in mind? Remember that income will be limited by the size of the space available to hold the event and by the number of prospects in your target audience.

Carefully consider what the cost per ticket would be. Are people in your area able and willing to spend that much? Local custom—that is the precedent that exists for fund-raising events in your area and for your institution—has a lot to do with whether your tickets will be coveted or shunned. In some locales, $100 per ticket is normal and acceptable; in others, $50 per ticket may price your event out of the market.

One successful event planner suggests using the cost of an evening out in your area, or in the nearest city, as a guide. She recommends tallying dinner and drinks at a first-class restaurant and entertainment, such as a play, concert, or dancing to a big-name band, and then adding 50 to 65 percent to this cost. If your projected ticket price is close to this mark, your chances for success are excellent. If the price is not in the ballpark, reconsider your plans or scale down by eliminating some extras such as custom-made favors or expensive flowers. A rule of thumb for fund-raising events is that expenses to stage the event should not exceed 30 percent of your total budget.

Support for fund-raising events builds over time. The first year for an event is not likely to be its biggest. The most successful fund-raising events have a track record and acquire a reputation as being the socially "in" thing to do. Therefore, in your first year, particularly if people in your area are not used to attending benefits, be conservative when you decide ticket prices—you can always raise them next year.

• • •

Budget Planning Checklist

When planning a special-events budget, take costs for the following items into account:

1. Facilities

❏ rental of meeting or reception room(s)

❏ overnight accommodations:

____ number of rooms _______ rate

❏ setup charges _________

❏ cleanup charges _________

Rental of:

❏ chairs

❏ props

❏ tent

❏ lighting

❏ coat checkroom

❏ additional telephone lines

❏ tables

❏ lectern

❏ canopy

❏ extra help

❏ electrical generators

2. Food service

- ❑ number of people to be served: ________
- ❑ the cost per person for:
- ❑ coffee breaks
- ❑ luncheon
- ❑ cocktail hour
- ❑ wine
- ❑ table linen
- ❑ rented table service (flatware and dishes)
- ❑ soda breaks
- ❑ dinner
- ❑ liquor
- ❑ other beverages
- ❑ gratuities
- ❑ test meal

3. Equipment rental

- ❑ tables
- ❑ flooring or carpeting
- ❑ ropes or stanchions
- ❑ registration desks and stools
- ❑ booths
- ❑ backdrop
- ❑ fencing
- ❑ canopy or tent
- ❑ risers
- ❑ props
- ❑ outdoor toilets
- ❑ lighting
- ❑ trash containers

4. Decor

- ❑ flowers
- ❑ extra plants
- ❑ corsages, boutonnieres
- ❑ direction signs
- ❑ table decorations
- ❑ props
- ❑ candles
- ❑ other decorations (ribbon, balloons)

5. Design and printing

- ❑ fee for design concept and package
- ❑ advance announcements
- ❑ programs
- ❑ posters
- ❑ maps
- ❑ signs
- ❑ name badges and holders
- ❑ invitations
- ❑ promotional fliers
- ❑ tickets
- ❑ placecards
- ❑ registration packets
- ❑ any other printed materials

6. Postage and shipping

- ❑ postage for invitations and reply cards
- ❑ mailing-house charges
- ❑ overnight shipping charges
- ❑ bulk mailing of promotional materials
- ❑ shipping

7. Recognition items

- ❑ awards, plaques, trophies
- ❑ calligraphy
- ❑ shipping and handling
- ❑ engraving
- ❑ framing

8. Miscellaneous

- ❑ VIP travel and expenses
- ❑ gifts
- ❑ extra help
- ❑ insurance
- ❑ taping and transcribing proceedings
- ❑ electrical connections
- ❑ cellular phone charges
- ❑ honoraria
- ❑ mementos
- ❑ security
- ❑ first-aid station
- ❑ visitors' center materials and staff
- ❑ water hookups

9. Transportation

- ❑ buses
- ❑ parking
- ❑ vans
- ❑ valets

10. Entertainment

- ❑ fees
- ❑ instrument rental
- ❑ promoter fees
- ❑ travel
- ❑ additional equipment
- ❑ rehearsal-time fees
- ❑ accommodations

11. Publicity

- ❑ advertising
- ❑ printed photos
- ❑ duplicating
- ❑ signs
- ❑ press-room equipment (computers, faxes, regular and modem phone lines)
- ❑ photographer
- ❑ slides
- ❑ mailing
- ❑ press-room hospitality
- ❑ banners

12. Audiovisual equipment

- ❑ slide and video projectors
- ❑ extension cords
- ❑ microphones
- ❑ speaker system
- ❑ pointers
- ❑ blackboards
- ❑ screens
- ❑ projector carts
- ❑ mixers
- ❑ tape recorders
- ❑ flip charts/markers
- ❑ technician services

13. Office expenses

- ❑ staff time
- ❑ data processing
- ❑ additional staff (students, temporaries)
- ❑ duplicating
- ❑ committee materials
- ❑ complimentary tickets
- ❑ staff travel and expenses
- ❑ overtime and compensatory time
- ❑ phones
- ❑ supplies (pens, pads, decals, folders)
- ❑ postage for general correspondence
- ❑ hospitality for committee members
- ❑ staff accommodations

CHAPTER 9

Follow Up!

WHEN THE EVENT IS OVER AND THE exhausted planner gazes out over drooping decorations, soiled tablecloths, and chairs in disarray, the work of tying up the special events package begins.

Before leaving the facility, secure or remove all valuables, such as audiovisual equipment, lecterns, microphones, easels, trophies, plaques, computers, and florals and other decorations that need to be saved or returned. Check for personal belongings that guests may have left behind. If the event was held in a hotel or other rented facility, the contract probably stipulates that all decorations and paraphernalia be removed from the property immediately. Anything left behind is likely to be discarded by the housekeeping staff.

• • •

On the First Working Day

On the first working day after an event, give immediate attention to follow-up publicity and write thank-you notes to all the people who helped make the event a success. This includes the speaker and all platform or dais participants, committee members, volunteers, the caterer, and the facility manager. If a student organization provided workers, send one note to the group's president to be shared at its next meeting. Sending thank-yous to the behind-the-scenes people, like university security, grounds crews, and the florist, will be much appreciated and will pave the way for good service in the future.

If it is your policy to issue refunds to people who paid but did not attend, do so immediately.

While they are still fresh, send leftover floral arrangements to high-traffic campus offices or to a local hospital or nursing home.

Telephone your committee chairperson and a sampling of other key people to get their reactions to the event and to thank them for participating.

Schedule a final committee meeting within the next two weeks. At the meeting, collect any bills and original office documents.

Return all rental equipment and check your own equipment to see that it has been properly cleaned and stored and that arrangements for any needed repairs have been made or replacements ordered.

While the details are fresh in your memory, write a chronological review of the event with comments about what was good and what was bad.

• • •

Within the Week

Follow up with your public affairs office to be sure that post-event publicity is being handled according to plan.

Submit all invoices to the financial officer responsible for paying bills. If bills are coming directly to you, verify the charges immediately and pay promptly. Check the arrangements orders from the caterer, florist, and other vendors to be sure they state the final number guaranteed and that any other changes to the original order are noted. Keep copies of all receipts and invoices for your records.

Prepare a final list of who was invited and who attended (also who reserved and didn't show up), and keep this list in your permanent file on the event. Share the information with other campus events planners. Bill any guest who attended but didn't pay.

• • •

Within a Month

For both cultivation and fund-raising events, prepare a follow-up report that describes every aspect of the event in detail. Refer to the original goals and objectives that you set in phase one of planning. Did the event meet its goals in friend raising, fund raising, and public relations? Did it draw the target audience? Was the intended message clearly and decisively delivered? If it was a cultivation event, did it provide enough information and foster enough good will so that when a development officer calls, the potential donor will be receptive to the request? What would you do differently next year? What would you do the same?

A financial report is essential for all events, but when the event was a fund raiser, this report is the acid test of whether or not you succeeded. It should include an income statement and a balance sheet and give the names and gift amounts of all donors.

If your analysis shows that the event did not meet its goals or did not generate the funds you had hoped for, find out why. The easiest way to accomplish this is simply to call people whom you can trust to give you an honest assessment.

Another important part of follow-up is to create and save a complete description of the event. This should include notes about the theme, the order of activities, the decorations, the facility, the program, the menus, the speakers, the publicity, the number of people who attended each segment, and a complete financial breakdown. Save copies of the invitations, programs, other printed materials, press releases, and clippings. Include comments about what worked and what didn't from your perspective as well as from that of committee members and guests. For major events such as an anniversary celebration or a building dedication, prepare a scrapbook and send a copy to the university archives for permanent storage. It is thoughtful to send VIP participants a copy of press clippings and any photographs of them taken during the event.

When a special event has been many months in the planning process and the committee has invested a great deal of time, it is appropriate (if the budget will allow) to invite members for cocktails or for an informal luncheon or brunch as a final thank-you. If a committee chair has been an especially devoted leader, a small gift that is reminiscent of the university or the event can be presented at this time.

Last, but not least, remember to thank your own staff and coworkers for their hard work.

• • •

Fund-raising Events Require an Action Follow-up

Planning for fund-raising follow-up should begin in the early days of an event's development. No event can be considered truly successful without effective follow-up. After all, whether an event is for cultivation or fund raising, its reason for being is to make money for the institution. Ironically, the lack of a solid plan for fund-raising followup is a common fund-raising mistake. Too often fund raisers are so relieved to have the event behind them that they are tempted to sit back and relax just when action is most needed, and they neglect to ask for the gift.

If an event is not followed up in a timely and appropriate fashion, the money and time invested in planning and holding it have been wasted. Failure to follow up is like writing and printing a direct-mail appeal but never mailing it.

While each event has a place in your development master plan, each event also has a life and time frame of its own. Therefore, each event requires a carefully crafted followup that will lead you and your constituents smoothly into the next step in the fund-raising plan.

At a Midwestern university, the campus center for the musical arts was nearing its 10th anniversary. When the center was built, an aggressive fund-raising campaign produced monies for enhancements such as a performance auditorium. Planners felt that the anniversary was an appropriate time to seek new donations for refurbishment and additional equipment. The development office special events planner created a cultivation event that would highlight the anniversary and the accomplishments of the previous 10 years, feature future goals, and lay the foundation for a fund drive.

The event was a success—or so it seemed. It was one of the highlights of the social season, it was well attended, and it received excellent media attention. Guests were entertained, wined and dined, and told about funding needs. But no money was ever raised as a result because no fund-raising followup had been planned. Because the fund raisers weren't ready to implement an action plan immediately following the event, the anniversary year passed and the opportunity to capitalize on it was lost.

During planning

Development strategies should take shape during the planning of an event. This is why event planners and development officers must work closely together. Development officers should have input about the guest list from the earliest days; should know who the corporate sponsors are; and already be working to find ways to reinforce the fund-raising message and to secure gifts. The development officer assigned to the event should craft any fund-raising messages to be delivered during the event and determine what fund-raising materials will be distributed.

After a cultivation event

Plans for fund-raising follow-up after a cultivation event should include these steps:

- Designating a development officer to be responsible for the process;
- Setting goals for the amount to be raised and a timetable to do it, including selecting dates for additional events if needed;
- Identifying prospects, including appropriate research into their giving histories and potentials;
- Assigning prospects to development officers;
- Planning for soliciting people who will not receive personal calls, including plans for direct mail or telephone follow-up; and
- Committing to see the drive through until all prospects have been contacted, receipts issued, thank-yous sent, and a final report filed.

In the case of the musical arts center, the development staffers should have had a well-conceived strategy with potential donors identified and supporting materials ready to go the following morning. They should have begun making calls and collecting pledges while the euphoria of a wonderful evening still lingered and the fund-raising message was fresh.

After a fund-raising event

Plans for followup after a fund-raising event should include these steps:

- Designating a development officer to be responsible for the process;
- Planning for meaningful ways to continue invloving the donors and volunteers who took part in the event;
- Researching the interests and giving potential of newcomers, including plans for nurturing their interest and building this involvement;
- Committing to ensure that gift receipting and acknowledgment procedures are followed properly and in a timely manner; and
- Adding the personal touch (extra phone calls or handwritten notes) that goes beyond standard institutional thank-you procedures for major individual and corporate sponsors and for volunteers.

• • •

Reinforcing Your Message with Special Follow-ups

Successful events open doors and establish relationships that no other public relations tool can. The chance to work together with people one-on-one through your volunteer network and to meet new people at the event itself affords a unique opportunity to build genuine, lasting friendships for your institution. The challenge after an event is to keep the doors open and the friendships growing.

Because volunteers and friends have made an emotional investment in a project they have helped support, keep them involved after the event is over by keeping them posted on the status of the project. If a fund-raising event raised money to construct a new facility, invite volunteers to a talk by the architect and a hard-hat inspection as soon as there is something to see. Remember to invite all volunteers and donors to events such as groundbreakings, dedications, and open houses. If your event raised funds for scholarships, invite the donors to an afternoon coffee with the scholarship students.

Host a volunteer appreciation party to thank those who helped and to give them a final report on the event. If you kept a scrapbook or photo album of the event, pass it around for all to enjoy. Such a gathering gives people a sense that the project had a beginning, a middle, and a conclusion and also serves as a primer to introduce the next event for which you will need their help. When you tell people the results of their hard work, you are also telling them that you respect the gifts of time and talent they have given.

Give each volunteer a small token of appreciation such as a memento of the event or of your campus; give individual recognition to key volunteers, and be lavish with thanks and praise for everyone.

If you cannot afford to host a gathering for volunteers, prepare a brief wrap-up letter and mail it to each person with a copy of a newspaper clipping and a handwritten thank-you in the margin.

Above all, don't let an entire year roll by before having further contact with these people. Find ways to stay in touch through mailings and invitations to other events so that you don't have to start from zero next year.

CHAPTER 10

Check and Double-check

MANY EVENT PLANNERS USE checklists to make sure everything has been arranged and nothing has been overlooked. Checklists are particularly helpful if for some reason the original planner is unable to attend the event. The lists provide a map to help a substitute step in and quickly learn all critical event details. Use the following sample forms as a basis for developing your own checklists. Here's what is included:

- Planning timeline
- Room-setup checklist
- Equipment checklist
- Audiovisual checklist
- Catering checklist
- Bar checklist
- Florist/decor checklist
- Program checklist
- Program participant/VIP checklist

Note: A budget planning checklist is included in Chapter 8.

• • •

Planning Timeline

Six months to a year ahead

- Select a theme
- Select the date, but before confirming it:
  - Clear the date with important participants;
  - Double-check for conflicts with major institutional, charity, or city functions;
  - Consider whether weather conditions or other demands on people's time (holidays, summer vacations, the start of school) might make that date inconvenient.

- Plan and get approval of a budget.
- Draw up a preliminary guest list.
- Select and reserve a facility.
- Develop a rain plan if the event is to be held outdoors.
- Reserve a block of hotel rooms, if necessary.
- Select and order recognition items and get them engraved immediately.
- Order favors, souvenirs, printed folders, and other giveaway items.
- Reserve special equipment such as vans, buses, tables, chairs, tents, and podiums.
- Audition entertainers.
- Plan audiovisual presentations and begin taking pictures to build a photo file for use in publications.
- Make preliminary security arrangements.
- Contact your risk manager to discuss insurance coverage.
- Get all necessary administrative approvals.
- Plan promotion and publicity.

Three to six months ahead

- Plan and get approval of printed invitations and all other printed materials.
- Finalize and get approval of the guest list.
- Select menus and submit them for approval.
- Print tickets and parking permits.
- Make contact with dais participants and
  - supply suggestions for their remarks;
  - gather their biographical information; and
  - request a professional photo of each participant for publicity and programs;
- Inform participants if academic regalia will be needed;
- Get their sizes and order for them if they do not have their own.
- Keep campus officials, deans, administrative officers, and local trustees (if appropriate) informed of your plans, and ask for their support.
- Confirm entertainment bookings.
- Plan the decorations and color scheme. Order props, special napkins, foods, or other unusual needs.
- Finalize the audiovisual presentations.
- Meet with the florist.
- Update security on your plans.
- Begin publicity, if appropriate.
- Send advance announcements to guest list, if appropriate.

Two months ahead

- Address invitations and set a mailing date.
- Finalize decorations and facility arrangements.
- Make hotel and transportation arrangements for out-of-town dignitaries.

- Mail an itinerary to dignitaries; include a reminder about bringing academic regalia (if needed).
- Double-check your academic regalia order.
- Secure hosts and hostesses and other university representatives to assist.
- Double-check the extra help that will be needed including valets, checkroom attendants, and greeters.
- Make direction and welcome signs.
- Write and print the program and menu cards (if needed).
- Get placecards lettered for everyone on the guest list.
- Check that any ceremonial items needed such as flags, the university mace, medals, toasting goblets, and the like can be located and that all are clean and in good repair.
- Check that flagpoles and stands are in working condition, and easels for displaying awards and seating charts are available, in working condition, and reserved for your use.
- Inspect the facility and request repairs to hazards that could cause an accident, such as loose edges on stairs and upturned edges on carpeting.
- Continue publicity on schedule.

Two to four weeks ahead

- Record and acknowledge RSVPs as they are received; send tickets, parking permits, and maps by return mail.
- Ask the grounds department to schedule a crew to mow and trim the grounds of the facility the day before your event. If your event will be held outdoors, request that the area be sprayed with insect killer.
- Take delivery on all printed materials.
- Stuff registration packets (if needed).
- If your event is taking place in another city, ship printed materials and other items to the meeting site. Call your contact person and ask how to label the shipment so that it will be accepted and not be misplaced on arrival.
- Double-check publicity progress with the public relations staff. Revise and update plans if necessary.
- Send detailed final instructions to all dignitaries with all tickets, parking permits, and maps. Supply them with the names and phone numbers of university officials and other VIPs who will be attending. Remember to include the full name of each VIP's spouse.
- Notify the caterer if the count seems to be significantly higher or lower than previously discussed.
- Write speeches and introductions, and get them approved.
- Take delivery on favors or mementos. Double-check for correct amount.
- Get table numbers made.
- Enlarge a diagram of the room to be used as seating chart.

One week ahead

- Ascertain the intentions of anyone who has not sent an RSVP.
- Print out the guest list in alphabetical order.
- Finish placecards.
- Make the seating chart.
- Brief the hosts and hostesses, greeters, and VIP escorts.
- Gather all presentation items such as gifts, plaques, trophies. Collect all ceremonial items.
- Put everything in a convenient, secure place, and designate one person to be in charge of transporting them to the event site.
- Plan an arrival briefing for VIPs if necessary.
- Call the university president's office and double-check for last-minute snags.
- Call security and double-check all arrangements. Provide them with final itineraries and VIP information.
- Send the guest list (with full names, titles, business and professional affiliations, and other specific interests), along with a final schedule of events, to the president, other academic officers, and official hosts.
- Deliver prepared introductions, citations, and speeches to those who will read them. Make extra copies for each person's secretary.
- Make catering guarantees.
- Have a university car filled with gas, cleaned, and placed on standby in case an emergency trip must be made to pick up a VIP or a forgotten item. Be certain the car has the appropriate parking permits for admission to all university lots.

The big day

- Arrive early.
- Have all the clothing and accessories with you that you will need for the entire day in case there is not time to go home to change.
- Have all instructions, directions, phone numbers, keys, extra parking permits, seating charts, and guest lists with you. Have your emergency kit along.
- Check all facilities and grounds. Pick up litter and spray for bugs if necessary.
- Assign one worker to be your assistant to stick close to you to run errands, send messages, and be on call for whatever need may arise.
- Relax and smile. Never tell "war stories" to your guests or intimate that things might be less than perfect. Chances are, no one but you will notice minor mistakes.

Room Setup Checklist

Date: ____________________________

Event title: ____

Date/time: ____

Institution sponsor: ____

Event planner: ____

Office phone: ______________________ Cellular phone: ___________________

Fax: ____

E-mail: ____

Address: ____

Facility name: ____

Address: ____

Facility manager: ____

Office phone: ______________________ Cellular phone: ___________________

Fax: ____

E-mail: ____

Rooms being used: ____

Caterer: ____

Contact person: ____

Office phone: ______________________ Cellular phone: ___________________

Room Setup Checklist

Florist: ______________________________

Contact person: ______________________________

Office phone: ________________ Cellular phone: ________________

Fax: ______________________________

E-mail: ______________________________

Specifications

Setups: ______________________________

Stage: ________________ Lights: ________________

Sound: ______________________________

Bandstand: ______________________________

Podium: ______________________________

Microphones (type needed): ______________________________

Number needed: ______________________________

Location of mikes: ______________________________

Bars and Serving areas

Bar needed: ________________ Location(s): ________________

Coat check room needed: ________________ Location: ________________

Registration area needed: ________________ Location: ________________

Floor plans

On a separate sheet, diagram the floor plan for each area to be used. Show setups for all areas; note traffic patterns and all entrances and exits. Attach.

Equipment Checklist

Date: ______________________

Event title: ______________________

Date/Time: ______________________

Institution sponsor: ______________________

Event planner: ______________________

Office phone: ______________ Cellular phone: ______________

Fax: ______________________

E-mail: ______________________

Address: ______________________

Facility name: ______________________

Address: ______________________

Facility manager: ______________________

Office phone: ______________ Cellular phone: ______________

Fax: ______________________

E-mail: ______________________

Rooms being used: ______________________

Times being used: ______________________

Rental company/On-campus source: ______________________

Address: ______________________

Contact person: ______________________

Office phone: ______________________

Equipment Checklist

Equipment needed and quantity: ____________________

____

____

____

Color scheme: ____________________

Cost: ____________________

Deposit required: ____________________

Balance due: ____________________

Delivery and setup instructions: ____________________

____

____

____

Pickup instructions: ____________________

____

____

Audiovisual Checklist

Date: ____________________

Event title: ____________________

Date/Time: ____________________

Institution sponsor: ____________________

Event planner: ____________________

Office phone: ____________________ Cellular phone: ____________________

Fax: ____________________

E-mail: ____________________

Address: ____________________

Facility name: ____________________

Address: ____________________

Facility manager: ____________________

Office phone: ____________________ Cellular phone: ____________________

Fax: ____________________

E-mail: ____________________

Rooms being used: ____________________

Equipment supplier: ____________________

Address: ____________________

Contact person: ____________________

Office phone: ____________________

Audiovisual Checklist

Check equipment needed:

❏ **Slide projectors:**
No. needed: ____________ For room: ____________ Time: ____________

❏ **Slide Trays:**
No. needed: ____________ For room: ____________ Time: ____________

❏ **Projector cart needed:** ❏ yes ❏ no
For room: ____________ Time: ____________

❏ **Extension cords:** ❏ Length: ____________
No. needed: ____________ For room: ____________ Time: ____________

❏ **Spare bulbs:** Size: ____________
No. needed: ____________ For room: ____________ Time: ____________

❏ **Screens:**
No needed: ____________ For room: ____________ Time: ____________

❏ **LCD projector:**
No. needed: ____________ For room: ____________ Time: ____________

❏ **Video projector:**
No. needed: ____________ For room: ____________ Time: ____________

❏ **Computer needed:** ❏ yes ❏ no
Kind: ____________
Software requested: ____________

❏ **Overhead projectors:**
No. needed: ____________ For room: ____________ Time: ____________

❏ **Microphones:** ❏ Type: ____________
No. needed: ____________ For room: ____________ Time: ____________

❏ **Tables:** ❏ Size: ____________
No. needed: ____________ For room: ____________ Time: ____________

❏ **Chairs:**
No. needed: ____________ For room: ____________ Time: ____________

❏ **Podiums:**
No. needed: ____________ For room: ____________ Time: ____________

❏ **Televisions:**
No. needed: ____________ For room: ____________ Time: ____________

Audiovisual Checklist

❑ **VCRs:**

No. needed: ____________ For room: ______________ Time: ____________

❑ **Flip charts:**

No. needed: ____________ For room: ______________ Time: ____________

Miscellaneous (check all that apply and note special instructions below):

❑ **Laser pointer** ❑ **Computer hookups**

❑ **Telephone** ❑ **Hand truck**

❑ **Extra extension cords** (specify length) ______________________________________

❑ **Other:** ____

Estimated cost: ____________ Amount of deposit: ________ Balance due: ________

Operator instructions: ____

____

____

Special instructions: ____

____

____

Equipment to be delivered on: Date: ______________ Time: ______________

Deliver to: ____

Equipment to be picked up on: Date: ______________ Time: ______________

Pickup instructions: ____

____

____

Catering Checklist

Date: ____________________

Event title: ____________________

Date/Time: ____________________

Institution Sponsor: ____________________

Event planner: ____________________

Office phone: ____________________ Cellular phone: ____________________

Fax: ____________________

E-mail: ____________________

Address: ____________________

Caterer: ____________________

Address: ____________________

Contact person: ____________________

Office phone: ____________________ Cellular phone: ____________________

Facility name: ____________________

Address: ____________________

Facility manager: ____________________

Office phone: ____________________ Cellular phone: ____________________

Rooms being used: ____________________

Time to serve: ____________________ Projected number of guests: __________

Date, time for final guarantee: ____________________

Catering Checklist

Cost per person: ____________________ Total projected cost: ________________

Deposit required: ____________________ Paid on date: ____________________

Balance due: ____

Menu: ____

____

____

____

Wines: ________________________ Toasting: ________________________

Linen colors: Napkins: ______________ Tablecloths: ____________________

Uniform for wait staff: ____

Placecards: ______________________ Menu cards: ______________________

Programs: ______________________ Favors: __________________________

Cocktails: ____

Time to serve: ____________________ Time to close: ___________________

Location(s) of bar(s): ____

Equipment to be supplied: ____

____

____

____

____

Bar Checklist

A well-stocked bar should have these supplies:

Alcoholic beverages

- ❑ vodka
- ❑ gin
- ❑ whiskey
- ❑ scotch
- ❑ bourbon
- ❑ rum
- ❑ beer, regular and light
- ❑ white wine
- ❑ dry vermouth
- ❑ red wine

Non-alcoholic beverages and mixes

- ❑ water
- ❑ soda water
- ❑ tonic water
- ❑ sparkling, flavored water
- ❑ tomato juice
- ❑ orange juice
- ❑ selection of soft drinks (including diet drinks)

Garnishes

- ❑ lemon and lime wedges
- ❑ cherries
- ❑ olives
- ❑ cocktail onions
- ❑ Angostura bitters
- ❑ sugar

Tools

- ❑ paring knife
- ❑ measuring spoons
- ❑ pitchers
- ❑ strainer
- ❑ jigger
- ❑ towels
- ❑ shaker
- ❑ can/bottle opener
- ❑ corkscrew
- ❑ cocktail napkins
- ❑ bartender's guide of drink recipes
- ❑ ice
- ❑ toothpicks
- ❑ ice tongs

Florist/Decor Checklist

Date: ____________________

Event title: ____________________

Date/Time: ____________________

Institution sponsor: ____________________

Event planner: ____________________

Office phone: ____________________ Cellular phone: ____________________

Fax: ____________________

E-mail: ____________________

Address: ____________________

Facility name: ____________________

Address: ____________________

Facility manager: ____________________

Office phone: ____________________ Cellular phone: ____________________

Rooms being used: ____________________

Florist: ____________________

Address: ____________________

Contact person: ____________________

Office phone: ____________________ Cellular phone: ____________________

Florist/Decor Checklist

Color scheme: ______________________________

Type of flowers ordered for: ______________________________

Tables: ______________________________

Dais: ______________________________

Reception area: ______________________________

Foyer: ______________________________

Corsages: ______________ Boutonnieres: ______________

Ushers/hosts/hostesses: ______________________________

Other: ______________________________

Time for deliveries: ______________________________

Containers to be returned: ______________________________

Rented equipment: ______________________________

Return by: ______________________________

Florist to pick up by: ______________________________

Other decorations: ______________________________

____

Supplier: ______________________________

Contact person: ______________________________

Office phone: ______________ Cellular phone: ______________

Special instructions: ______________________________

____

Program Checklist

Date: ______________________

Event title: ______________________

Date/Time: ______________________

Institution sponsor: ______________________

Event planner: ______________________

Office phone: ______________ Cellular phone: ______________

Fax: ______________________

E-mail: ______________________

Address: ______________________

Facility name: ______________________

Address: ______________________

Facility manager: ______________________

Office phone: ______________ Cellular phone: ______________

Rooms being used: ______________________

Program content: ______________________

Honored guests/VIPs: ______________________

Musicians/Band: ______________________

Contact person: ______________________

Office phone: ______________________

Address: ______________________

Time to begin: ______________ Time to end: ______________

Time to set-up: ______________________

Fee: ____________________ Deposit paid: ____________________

Check needed at performance: __________ Yes: __________ No: __________

Amount: ____________________ Pay to: ____________________

Master of ceremonies: ____________________

Office phone: ____________________ Cellular phone: ____________________

Address: ____________________

Speakers: ____________________

Name: ____________________ Name: ____________________

Address: ____________________ Address: ____________________

Office phone: ____________________ Office phone: ____________________

Audiovisuals to be used: ____________________

Equipment supplied by: ____________________

Contact person: ____________________

Office phone: ____________________

Address: ____________________

Program Participant/VIP Checklist

Date: ____________________________

Event title: ____

Date/ Time: ____

Institution sponsor: ____

Event planner: ____

Office phone: ______________________ Cellular phone: ___________________

Fax: ____

E-mail: ____

Address: ____

Facility name: ____

Address: ____

Facility manager: ____

Office phone: ______________________ Cellular phone: ___________________

Rooms being used: ____

Participant's name: ____

Title/Affiliation: ____

Office address: ____

Home address: ____

Office phone: ______________________ Home phone: ____________________

Fax: ____

Program/Participant Checklist

E-mail: ____________________

Secretary's name: ____________________

Contact person: ____________________

Office (area code/phone): ____________________

Home (area code/phone): ____________________

Audiovisual requirements: (List equipment needed. If none, state "none.")

____

____

____

Academic regalia:

❑ Will furnish own ❑ Need to order:

Gown size: __________ Cap size: __________ Colors: __________

To receive: ❑ Award ❑ Medal Plaque ❑ Citation ❑ Honorary degree

❑ Other: ____________________

Presentation item ordered: __________ From: __________

Travel Plans: ____________________

Arrival date: __________ Time: __________

Driving: ____________________

Flight (airport/airline/flight number and time): ____________________

To be met by: ____________________

Meeting place: __________ Time: __________

Program/Participant Checklist

Accommodations:

Hotel name: ______________________________

Address: ______________________________

Phone: ______________________________

Dates of reservations: ______________________________

Special requests: ______________________________

Departure:

Date: ______________ Time: ______________

Flight (airport/airline/number/time): ______________________________

To be escorted by: ______________ Phone: ______________

Will meet for departure at: ______________________________

Expenses:

❑ To be paid by participant ❑ To be reimbursed, receipts required

❑ To be paid by: ______________________________

Address: ______________________________

Account number or billing information: ______________________________

Honorarium to be paid: $______________ Budget: ______________

Other needs:

Special diet: ______________________________

Non-smoking accommodations: ______________________________

Handicapped parking/seating: ______________________________

Is spouse accompanying? ______________ If so, name: ______________

CHAPTER 11

Basic Events to Go

THERE ARE CERTAIN STANDARD EVENTS—recognition ceremonies, retirements, ribbon cuttings, and the like—and classic questions (what is event's role in a capital campaign, how are independent planners hired and paid)—that every event planner encounters. Here are the how-to basics of several of types of standard events and answers to common questions. These directions are easy to follow. Just add enthusiasm!

• • •

Presenting a Rewarding Ceremony

Spring's steady fare of award and scholarship presentations, recognition ceremonies, and faculty and staff retirements presents challenges.

One question is how to plan a ceremony that is dignified and meaningful without being boring.

Space presents another dilemma. For some, the challenge is making large auditoriums seem filled and intimate. For others, the problem is improvising a stage, lighting, and audience seating in a ballroom, conference room, or on the campus green.

Perhaps the worst problem: finding ways to entice people to sit up front so that speakers aren't addressing an empty first five rows.

Focus on the winners

Awards ceremonies often get a quick brush off from planners because they fall into the realm of the routine and they happen during the busy spring season, but for the honorees and their families these are very special occasions. Receiving an award may be a career highlight or the only recognition a person ever receives for his or her efforts. It's important to remember that the people being recognized are the reason for the gathering, and the focus should remain squarely on them.

Stage it

Begin planning by visiting the facility you will use and trying to view it with fresh eyes and an open mind. Take a seat in the back of the room looking toward the stage to understand the audience's point of view. Recall previous years' ceremonies, and consider what worked, what didn't and why.

Make careful notes of aisles, stairs onto the stage, curtains, lighting, and sound capabilities. While the set you create may be minimal, avoid decorating the stage with only a battered podium partially hidden by a large flower arrangement. Instead, think of ways to make the stage look filled and colorful.

One inexpensive technique is to use theater lights fitted with colored gels that shine beams onto background curtains or a blank wall. The intense lights can wash large areas with bright colors, giving depth and hiding empty, dark corners. If you are using a ballroom or meeting room where lights can't be hung, accomplish the same effect by placing lights on the floor and shining the beams upward onto a wall. Plan to use a spotlight on the podium. One way to highlight the honored guests and provide inexpensive decor is to project their photos onstage as their names are called. Use a professional photographer to take slides of people in their everyday environments. For major award winners, tape very short video interviews. Both of these techniques lend visual interest to the stage and are fun and flattering for the winners.

Another way to fill the stage is to use it to seat the honorees. Placing recipients onstage also helps make the ceremony flow because winners don't have to walk to the stage to receive their awards. Fill in with a combination of tall plants, such as ficus trees, and shorter plants, such as peace lilies and large potted ferns. Work with the theater department to light the stage so that everyone can be seen. Other useful props that may be stashed in storage are classic Greek columns or busts of famous writers, musicians, scientists, or other scholars.

If you will be building a stage in a ballroom or conference room, make a platform using risers that are 16 or 24 inches high. If the room is very big and you are expecting a large crowd, consider building a 36-inch-tall platform. You will need sturdy portable stairs with handrails so that people can walk on and off the platform safely. Use skirting to hide the risers' metal legs, and set large potted plants near the edge to soften the look and make the edge is visible to participants.

Be efficient

A well-managed awards ceremony should not last longer than one hour. To accomplish this, script the entire program and then use staff to do a walk through, timing each element as you go. Trim as needed by rethinking the way things have always been done and taking new approaches. For example, is it necessary to have the dean give a 20-minute speech? How about switching to a five-minute talk? Do three soloists need to perform? How about reducing it to one?

In many awards ceremonies much time is wasted waiting while each recipient makes his or her way from the audience to the podium. You can solve this and incorporate a flourish into the ceremony by having all of the winners proceed to the stage at the beginning of the program. To do this, seat the audience, then have the honorees march to music from the back of the room to the stage. The winners then take assigned seats on stage for the duration.

Another approach is to have winners lined up offstage with a staff member cuing them to walk on at the appropriate time. After receiving the award, each winner walks off stage to a seat in the front row of the audience to enjoy the rest of the program.

No matter how close at hand the winners may be, it is a good idea to use music or narration to fill the pause and cover the clomping of footsteps as each recipient makes his or her way to the podium.

Other ways to pare are eliminating unnecessary speakers, multiple introducers, and extraneous entertainment and preventing long-winded acceptance speeches.

Script it

To ensure success, write a script for the entire program including cues for the speakers, winners, musicians, and lighting and sound technicians. Then designate an emcee to read all introductions and move the program smoothly from item to item.

This eliminates a major time-wasting pitfall: allowing many people to access the microphone. Using multiple introducers can be risky because some will envision themselves at the Academy Awards ceremony and ramble on forever, while others will arrive unprepared and try to wing it.

Scripting evens the amount of material presented about each person and ensures a consistent format. Begin work on your script well in advance by collecting biographical information on all honorees. The same information can be used for a printed program. While the emcee reads, department representatives can place the award in the winner's hands and escort him or her on stage; the only difference is that the representative is not given a speaking part.

If honorees are to give a response, limit them to one minute and know that they will likely speak for three. Tell them they will be cued when time is up, and do so by signaling from the front row of the audience by flicking on a small colored flashlight. Give the speaker 30 seconds more to conclude. At that point, the music can come up or the emcee can interject a thank-you.

Practice makes perfect

A few days in advance, send participants reminders that include information about dress, when and where the ceremony will be held, and how long it is expected to take. Schedule a rehearsal to begin about 45 minutes before guests arrive. This is a good opportunity to determine if everyone has shown up and to briefly explain the program order. Let people practice walking onto the stage and speaking into the microphone if necessary. Label chairs with note cards so participants know where to sit. To ensure that no ink from the labels transfers to clothing, use wide, clear packing tape to cover the lettering. This technique is also useful for marking standing positions on stage. Simply tape the card to the floor where the person should stand.

Practice tricky moves such as placing medals around people's necks or presenting heavy trophies. Clearly mark all plaques and other awards so that the presenter doesn't mix them up.

Down in front

Just how do you get people to sit in the front? Set out fewer chairs than the number of guests you expect, thus forcing people to use all available places. Have additional seating readily available to be brought out should the need arise.

If you are using an auditorium with far more seats than needed, try using some or all of these techniques.

First, block off access to balconies and upper levels with cording until the entire lower level is filled.

Use ushers to escort people to seats, filling the room from the front to the rear.

Use cording or ribbon to block rear seats or entire seating sections. Open them later if necessary.

Assign VIP seating in the front for families, scholarship donors, university officials, and any other group you choose. Give them tickets in advance or use a simple color-coded system to direct them. For example, tell them their seats are in the blue section and mark the ends of the corresponding rows with blue bows. Be certain the ushers know your system.

• • •

Farewell to Faculty and Friends

Looking for that perfect recognition item for faculty, staff, or board retirements? Here are some ideas and resources to get you started.

Classics

Gifts in this group are the campus equivalents of gold watches.

Chairs. Fine handcrafted wooden chairs, usually in rocker or Windsor styles, these generally come in a dark finish, sometimes with cherry arms, and feature your campus logo or seal on the chair back.

Solid silver Revere bowls. Pricey, impractical, yet popular, silver bowls can be engraved and are beautiful for home or office. Try the fine jewelry department of your local department store or a flatware store at your local outlet mall. If sterling is a little out of range, attractive 10-inch engravable silverplate Revere bowls are readily available.

Plates. Commission a heritage plate custom-painted with your campus scenes.

Paperweights. Hand-blown glass paperweights that incorporate campus colors or that have your seal embedded are lovely and unique. Have them produced by local art students or faculty or glassblowers who work in the demonstration areas of historic villages or theme parks.

Crystal. Apples (the symbolic gift for teachers), paperweights, bowls, candlesticks, boxes, and sculptures are always in good taste.

Personally yours

Looking for something that is unique to your campus? Try these suggestions:

Prints. Commission a print of an original watercolor, drawing, or photograph of a campus landmark.

Sculpture or ceramics. Produce a signature piece to be given exclusively for recognition. Use student or faculty artists.

Pens. Fine writing instruments are always a welcome gift. Order them personalized with your logo reproduced in jewelry-quality, die-struck, or silk-screened emblems applied to the pen clip or imprinted on the pen cap or barrel. The pens can be also be engraved.

Here are some additional suggestions: engraved or imprinted bookends, mantle clocks, desk lamps, handcrafted pins. One institution's pin is produced in sterling silver by a local artist and is a replica of the campus' signature columns. A professional photo of the entire board, staff, or the retiree with the university president, framed and personalized with a message.

To help retirees remain connected with campus activities and keep out-of-pocket recognition costs to a minimum, try these suggestions:

- a scholarship for continuing education courses;
- a lifetime membership at the school's golf course or health facility;
- a lifetime campus parking permit;
- complimentary passage for two on an alumni tour to a fabulous destination;
- the use of office space for a set period of time;
- an honorary top-level lifetime membership in a giving society that will provide a constant flow of attractive perks and invitations;
- lifetime tickets to campus theatre or concert series or season tickets to the person's favorite sport.

Making the presentation

Most institutions say farewell to retiring faculty and staff at a dinner, dessert, tea, or reception. Board members are typically feted at their final meeting. The format you choose is not important—any of these will work. What is important is to plan the event for a day and time when the majority of people who would like to take part can be present. Consider hosting retirements at times when a crowd is already on campus for other reasons, such as commencement or spring reunion weekend, or around honors convocations.

If you have good photo archives, a fun way to decorate that is sure to generate conversation is by displaying old photographs. Look for pictures taken at different points in the retirees' careers and have the photos enlarged, mounted, and exhibited at the event. Get the memories flowing by including old photos of campus scenes, former presidents and deans, and major campus happenings.

Ask retirees well in advance for personal guest lists, and mail formal invitations. Use a local news release, coverage in the alumni magazine, and an announcement on your Web site to give as many people as possible the opportunity to send cards, flowers, or other greetings.

Place a story or advertisement announcing all retirees in the alumni magazine and local newspaper. Put the same information on your Web site.

• • •

Celebrate No Matter How You Cut It

A ribbon cutting signals the completion of a large project that likely took years to accomplish. But while the ceremony marks the start of something new, it is also a time to tie together past and future, to recognize and thank the people who had a part in making the new building a reality, and to show off the facility to special guests and the public.

Here are some tips for making your ribbon cutting interesting and purposeful.

Remember your friends

Build a VIP guest list of people who helped make the project a reality. Because buildings are often years in planning and construction, carefully research those who were instrumental in the early phases but who may no longer be involved. Examples include the relatives of the deceased donor whose bequest made the building possible, a past university president, a former representative who shepherded an appropriation through the state legislature, retired faculty and staff, and a former member of the college board of trustees.

Get coverage

One of the key goals of a ribbon cutting is publicity, so plan the ceremony with the media in mind. This means creative visuals and a schedule that is convenient for news crews. Hold your ceremony between 10 a.m. and 3 p.m. for the best chance of winning a spot on the evening news. Boost your chances for coverage by selecting a day of the week that is typically a slow news day. Local assignment editors can tell you which days are best bets in your community.

Instead of just cutting a ribbon at the front door, think in terms of color, movement, and creativity. Planners have used ribbon-cutting robots and laser beams to do the honors. One worked with students well in advance to create a Rube Goldberg type ribbon-cutting device.

To salute the community effort required to make her university's new arts facility a reality, one planner invited several hundred people to cut the dedication ribbon. She wrapped a giant ribbon around the building's perimeter. Guests, who were each given a pair of small scissors, took places around the building and, at a signal, simultaneously snipped the ribbon.

At one university, a plastic strip of DNA substituted for a traditional ribbon when the school's science building was dedicated.

However you slice it, make sure the action can easily be seen by the audience by elevating dignitaries on a stage equipped with adequate sound and lighting. Rope off an area for the media.

Hang the ribbon at mid-chest height so it is easier to frame in photos or videos.

Work with campus news service

Get the word out in advance to the media through your campus news service. On ribbon-cutting day, welcome and accommodate reporters and crews with special parking, packets of background information, and adequate technical arrangements, such as sufficient power and lighting and enough room to set up a three-person crew. Offer a private room for interviews with VIPs.

Advance information should include credentials or tickets, maps of how to find the facility, where to park, and maps of the building's interior. Note the locations of essentials like phones and restrooms.

Script it

To be certain the content of the ceremony is meaningful, designate a master of ceremonies and write a script that incorporates your public relations messages and includes the names of all dignitaries who will be recognized from the platform. Speakers should be limited to three and should talk for a maximum of five minutes each. Brevity is especially critical if the audience will be standing.

Think safety

Often, construction crews are still putting the finishing touches on new facilities for weeks after the ribbon is cut. Check the area where visitors will be permitted to identify possible tripping hazards, grates where high heels could get caught, construction debris, dangling wires, and the like. Clearly mark areas that are off limits. Make arrangements for non-skid floor mats inside of doors if the building's permanent mats have not been installed.

It's cut. Now what?

Immediately after the cutting, invite guests to tour the facility. Students and faculty—who can serve as guides, answer questions, and give demonstrations—make tours more meaningful. Strategically locate refreshments in an area that encourages people to walk through the building.

Limit access to the building's interior until after the ribbon-cutting program. If it's a blustery day, consider serving hot beverages to the audience waiting for festivities to begin; otherwise, reserve the food until after the program.

As guests depart, it is particularly nice to give them a souvenir. This can be a printed program, a photograph, or a piece of the cut ribbon mounted in a card that describes the building, the donor (if applicable), and the dedication date.

Snippets

Entertain the crowd with live music before the ceremony begins.

Use ribbon-cutting day to showcase student talent by involving students as hosts and hostesses, asking them to speak, or having them set up displays inside the facility.

If you cannot provide seating for everyone, set up and reserve a small number of chairs for persons who are unable to stand.

Ask people to sign a guest book that can be placed in the university archives or included in a dedication-day time capsule.

Ask dignitaries to remain on stage for photos immediately following the ceremony.

Prop houses may have large scissors for rent.

Avoid a sour ending by arranging to have police direct traffic.

Devise a rain plan, which might be as simple as a canopy, lots of umbrellas, or an alternative date. For the dedication of one school's engineering building, one institution held its ribbon cutting across the street inside the creative arts center. A giant picture of the new building was projected on stage, and a ribbon in the school colors of gold and blue was stretched across the screen. VIPs cut the ribbon while guests looked on in auditorium comfort.

• • •

Summer is Tee Time

Tee up a golf tournament to raise funds and friends, and to attract people who do not respond to other invitations. There are more than 25 million golfers in the United States. Regular players often participate in golf events as a way to play different courses. And the sport's growing popularity with women has made golf tournaments popular fund raisers for women's on-campus programs, especially in athletics.

Golf tournaments typically attract a cross-section of people, from novices to those who take the game very seriously and expect every detail to be according to the rule book. Here are some tips for planning a basic, just-for-fun golf event.

People are attracted by the opportunity to play a unique or prestigious course, especially one that is not open to the public.

Contact the course early. Many courses book far in advance and allow tournaments only on days they are closed to members. To gain access to some private clubs, you may have to find a member to sponsor your group.

Mondays and Wednesdays are good days for tournaments; Fridays are not. Clubs usually will not consider a weekend date. Before deciding on a date, check other clubs and charitable organizations to be sure another golf tournament or significant social event is not scheduled at the same time. Once you pick the date, notify all golf pros in your area and ask them to put it on their club's golfer's calendar of upcoming regional events.

Carefully consider time of day. Morning tournaments appeal to many people because they can play and go back to work after lunch. Parents with school-age children prefer a morning format because it doesn't disrupt after-school, dinner-time, and homework routines. A good time to begin is about 9 a.m.

Learn about other tournaments in your area, especially those sponsored by charities. If you live where there are lots of tournaments, be competitive in pricing and amenities.

Decide whether you will offer entertainment for nonplayers. Nongolfer activities, such as a special program on campus or a visit to area tourist attractions, can help sell tickets, especially if the tournament involves lots of out-of-town visitors (during reunion weekend, for example). Include tickets for the social hour and dinner with this package. Provide transportation from the course and back via university van or bus.

Arrange the mechanics of play through the golf-course pro. Meet with the pro often so you know what services (arranging pairings, assigning carts, and posting scores) the pro will provide. He or she can also offer a wealth of planning information about what works and what doesn't. At some courses, there is a $1 to $3 per-player fee for this service.

Food service arrangements are made through the club's food and beverage manager.

Use caution with course contracts; many stipulate guarantee dates and carry stiff cancellation penalties.

To determine registration fees, include costs for printing and mailing a flier, greens fees, cart fees (figure two people per cart; therefore divide the cost of the cart by two and charge each person that amount), range balls (for warming up), prizes (if purchasing), complimentary guests, food and beverage service, refreshment service on the course, and any extras (such as entertainment or equipment rental).

Mail invitations about six weeks ahead. Close registrations at least one week ahead to have time to assign teams and make guarantees.

Look beyond your alumni list for potential participants. Opening your tournament to all, especially if it is a fund-raiser, increases the likelihood of selling all playing spots and can attract new dollars. Ask golf pros at other courses in your area if you can post your tournament announcement on locker-room bulletin boards.

Require check-in at a registration table. You will need a minimum of two workers at this table. Tell golfers the hole where they will start (give them the number in writing), tag their bags with this number, and have their bags taken to the corresponding cart. This is also the time to give golfers a course map, a copy of the rules, and a list of prize holes.

Give golfers a tee bag filled with tees, visors, ball towels, balls and the like. The more of these items with your campus logo, the better; however, local businesses will usually donate tee-bag items that carry their logos.

Before play begins, gather all golfers for a brief welcome. Have the pro explain the tournament rules.

Make play fun by declaring certain holes prize holes. State the challenge—such as closest to the pin, shortest drive, longest putt—on signs at each hole's tee box.

Begin play with a shotgun start. This means teams simultaneously tee off from every hole. It eliminates the need for tee times and enables everyone to finish at about the same time—figure four and a half hours to play 18 holes.

Provide beverages on the course either from coolers left at tee boxes or from a cart driven by two workers who roam the course throughout play. Handy extras for the cart are sunscreen, a first-aid kit, and a walkie-talkie or cellular phone. Build the cost of two beverages per person into the tournament fee so that people do not have to bother with cash during play.

Plan a brief awards program that runs efficiently. You will need a sound system, especially if you are outside.

Have the post-play social hour and prizes ready as soon as golfers finish, or many will head for their cars. To ensure that people stay, entice them early in the day with the promise of door prizes, good food, and fun. If a message is to be delivered by the university president or other official, keep it light and short, and schedule it before the prize presentation. If the course doesn't have a clubhouse facility, set up a tent on site instead of requiring people to drive to another location. Otherwise, people who know they aren't receiving a prize are likely to go home. Players are more likely to leave quickly following morning tournaments because many need to get back to their offices.

If you are serving a meal after play, make arrangements for golfers to use club showers and changing rooms.

For prizes, give campus logo items such as coffee mugs, golf shirts, pen and pencil sets, and hats. When giving shirts or other apparel, have a wide selection of sizes and a sufficient quantity of each on hand so that you can give each winner his or her correct size on the spot. Try to get expensive prizes donated. Remember that for team awards, you will need four or five identical prizes, one for each member of the team. First, second, and third prizes are usually something substantial like golf bags, drivers, or a gift certificate to the club's pro shop. Season tickets to events on campus or high-quality logo items would also be welcome.

Recruit a volunteer host committee to staff the registration table, manage prize holes, fill coolers, retrieve signs from the course, hand out prizes, and relay messages. Don't commit yourself to remaining in a particular location; you need to be free to respond to situations as they arise.

Your tournament will grow each year provided people have fun and everyone gets something to take home as a memento of the day.

Have a rain plan

Decide early in the planning process how the possibility of bad weather will be handled. Policies about this should be in writing and given to golfers before they register.

Will you choose a rain date? If people can't play that day, are they eligible for a refund?

Provide golfers with a phone number to call in case of foul weather on tournament day to learn whether play will be held. If rain begins during play but there is no lightning, many golfers will continue. If, however, there is lightning in the area, the course must be cleared. The pro will usually make this determination, and with the course marshal will require players to return to the clubhouse until the storm passes. It is a good idea to have something planned to fill this time, for example:

- Have refreshments ready (preferably complimentary) including beverages and snacks.

- Provide entertainment such as golf instructional videos shown on a big-screen television.
- Invite the club pro or your institution's coaches to give a brief presentation until the weather clears.

Know the locations of telephones so that people can use the time to make calls.

Determine policies in advance for handling the possibility of having to call off or shorten the tournament once play has begun.

Research the club's cancellation policies before signing contracts, and consider cancellation insurance.

Fun formats to consider

Night Golf

A popular golf event currently sweeping the country is night golf. Strictly for fun, night golf is not a real golf tournament. This format can attract people who are drawn by its novelty. The format offers flexibility in scheduling because golfers don't tee off until after dusk.

Players are given glow-in-the-dark golf balls (ask the pro how to order) and divided into pairs, usually of men and women. Players alternate hitting shots and try to sink the ball in the cup with the fewest number of shots. The game becomes more challenging (and funny) as the darkness increases.

Play is slow, so plan to play only about four holes. Provide players with (or ask them to bring) flashlights and lightweight jackets.

Start the evening with a cookout and conclude with nightcaps, hors d'oeuvres, and prizes. Give prizes for the lowest score and for silly things like the highest score, greatest number of wiffs, and most putts.

A Scramble

A scramble is a fun and easy-to manage tournament format.

In a scramble, players are divided into teams of four or five individuals, without regard to players' golf handicaps. You can build the teams, or golfers can register to play with their friends. The object of a scramble is to be the team with the lowest score at the end of 18 holes.

To play, each golfer on the team hits a shot. Team members then select the ball they consider to be in the best position for the next shot. Players move their balls to that spot and hit again. The process is repeated until the ball is in the hole. This removes the pressure to perform and allows skillful and weak golfers to play together and still have a good time.

At the end of play, the team with the lowest score wins. Prizes are awarded for the winning team and for a variety of both funny and serious accomplishments, like the longest drive, the closest to the pin on a particular hole, the shortest drive, most times in the water, the longest putt, a hole-in-one, and the highest score.

• • •

Auction Basics

Fund-raising auctions are more popular than ever and, when properly managed, will yield handsome annual dividends for your cause. The most successful auctions are built around a few basic rules.

First, invite prominent people. Set your sights high, and concentrate on inviting people who can afford to spend $50 to $75 per ticket. These are the people with disposable income. If your auction is frequented by bargain hunters instead of generous patrons interested in helping a charitable cause, it's time to upgrade your guest list.

Second, offer quality items. Think about the things prominent people buy, and get those items into the sale. The number-one sellers are ego items, like vacation packages that include transportation and posh accommodations, autographed memorabilia, and other things one can't buy in a store, such as the naming of a street on campus for a person or corporation, dinner with the university president, or the opportunity to serve as headmaster for a day.

Third, hire a quality auctioneer. Choose a professional who has been to auctioneer's school and who knows how to control the crowd, entertain the audience, and secure the highest possible bids.

Auction planning should begin a year in advance. One of the first steps is to make lists of potential committee members, guests, and items for sale.

Choose a theme. A theme really adds to the auction making it more fun. Oriental, Western, and Hawaiian themes are popular, and it's easy to find suitable items. Consider, for example, offering a dude-ranch vacation at a Western theme auction.

Hold the live auction in a brightly lighted room during dinner. This helps bidding because people are in their seats and not going anywhere. Brighter lighting helps people see who else is bidding and can lead to friendly competition and bidding wars.

Another trend is finding corporate sponsors to underwrite the event's expenses so that all monies raised can go to charitable purposes.

One common mistake is waiting to sell the auction's most desirable item until last. Instead, think of the sale as following a bell-shaped curve. The first five or six live-auction items should be of general interest, like televisions or bicycles that will sell quickly and bring a good price. This sets the pace and gets the crowd interested.

Next, the auctioneer should start inserting some bigger-ticket items as a prelude to the featured, most expensive item. The auctioneer should gradually bring the sale back to popular, general-interest merchandise so that it ends on a positive note. Selling the big-ticket item in the middle prevents people from passing on items all evening in anticipation of that special thing, only to lose it. Auctioning the premier item early frees people to bid on other merchandise.

Here are some additional tips:

- Have other fun things going on like booths and games where people can win prizes. Set up duck ponds and balloon pops, and sell keys that might open a treasure chest; keep things lively and let everyone have fun.
- Served meals work better than buffets because they keep people in their seats during the live auction.
- For silent auctions, post minimum bids and raises to avoid having people bidding in increments of $1 or less. Expect to get at least 75 percent of an item's retail value.
- Add a super silent auction grouping merchandise that are of higher value and could be part of the live auction but that have limited appeal. An example would be thousands of dollars of orthodontic work donated by a local dentist. Make a special display of these items, and ask the auctioneer to promote it during the live auction.
- To keep bidding lively and people engaged, don't start the live auction later than 7:00 or 8:00 p.m., and don't go longer than two hours. (Auctioneers generally cover 30 items per hour.)
- Don't disrupt the live auction's momentum by taking a break or letting amateur auctioneers have the mike.
- Don't lull the crowd with speeches before the sale starts.
- Keep the silent auction open during the live auction and dinner, but close all games. Gradually close the silent auction so that it is shut completely by the time the live auction ends.
- Print a catalog of items for sale, and mail it to ticket holders about 10 days in advance. This gives people time to decide what they want and may also generate additional ticket sales. Sell catalog advertising to people like attorneys and insurance agents who don't have an items to donate, but who might want to support your cause. Print and send an inexpensive teaser flier to members of your target audience who have not purchased tickets.
- Avoid loading the live auction with expensive items that require minimum bids to sell. These items (for example, a pair of snowmobiles that require a minimum bid of $8,000) are really consignments, not donations. If you offer items with minimum bids, be sure they will bring a profit of at least $500.
- Hold a drawing for something extra special at the end of the evening to keep people from leaving early.
- Announce next year's auction date before guests depart.

• • •

Events to Enhance Travel Program

Almost every alumni association sponsors a travel program. Here's how to plan events that will help you get the most PR mileage from yours.

Bon voyage

Pre-departure gatherings are the perfect way to launch alumni travelers on a successful journey and to involve them more closely with your institution.

Held about two weeks before departure, a weekday luncheon is a nice way to give participants the chance to meet one another and the official escort, to hear a formal presentation about the destination, and to ask questions.

The briefing also provides the chance for alumni association staff to renew acquaintances with travelers, to update them on the university, and to give a campus tour.

Luncheon should be paid for by the alumni association, and it is also nice to provide travelers a special gift. Things like luggage tags or a pouch filled with travel-sized toiletries imprinted with your logo are nice.

Ask a faculty member to brief passengers on cultural and political topics, weather, and communication facilities.

All aboard

Once at the destination or on board ship, treat travelers to a private reception to help people start to get acquainted and build camaraderie.

After arrival

At the destination, invite alumni living in the country to join the travelers for dinner. This serves as an alumni event for people living in foreign countries and provides travelers the benefit of getting tips from people who actually live in the region.

Travel reunion time

Once a year, invite the past year's travelers to campus again, this time for a travel reunion.

People can bring their photos and share their memories. What's more, they can browse the displays set up by tour operators to preview the coming travel season's destinations.

If your travel program is large, ask tour operators to attend at their own expense and help underwrite the cost of food and beverage.

Here are some additional tips for tour briefings:

- Serve foods of the destination country during luncheons or receptions.
- Help set the mood with inexpensive decorations from a party supply store.
- Play recordings of the country's native music.
- When sponsoring the same trip on consecutive years, invite travelers from the previous year to mingle with guests and share their insights and enthusiasm.
- Provide a list of suggested reading material, including travel guides, articles from travel magazines, and Internet addresses of useful information.
- People love to talk about their vacations: About a month after the tour returns, invite the travelers to campus to reminisce and show off their photos.

• • •

Positioning Events For Capital Campaign Success

Capital campaigns seem to be everywhere, and events play an important role in their success. Capital campaigns usually begin with an institutional self-study that produces a set of campaign goals. These ideas are submitted to the trustees, faculty, staff, students, alumni, and friends in what is known as a feasibility study. The campaign's first events are likely to occur during this period.

Similar to focus groups but conducted on a larger scale, feasibility-study events are usually small meetings held around dinners or luncheons in different cities and with different constituents. Speakers make presentations about your school and the proposed capital campaign. Participant reactions and advice then help determine whether the proposals are on track.

If feasibility results are positive, the campaign's public relations and development planning begin in earnest. The fund-raisers name the target audiences, set dollar goals for each, and establish a timetable for solicitation. This timetable becomes the guide for events scheduling.

Campaign themes are developed during this planning period. Like an advertising slogan, a campaign theme should encapsulate the main idea of the campaign's purpose and motivate people to give. The theme appears in all messages, whether written, spoken, or delivered through events, and figures greatly in the types of events sponsored. Special campaign logos and colors may be chosen that should also be incorporated into event invitations, decorations, and printed materials.

Kickoff

The kickoff event is the campaign's coming out party. It is the first time the campaign is announced publicly, and it heralds the beginning of a high-profile time of heightened activity. By the time kickoff occurs, the fund raisers will have been quietly working behind the scenes for months to secure major donor commitments. In fact, by kickoff, you may be a year or more into the campaign schedule, and as much as 80 percent of the goal may already be pledged.

Kickoff is a public relations focal point because it unveils goals and objectives and gets the popular bandwagon rolling. The kickoff event usually coincides with a special weekend (like reunions) or day (such as founder's day) when lots of people will be on campus. Because of this, the kickoff event is often part of a cluster of smaller events that may or may not be campaign related.

A kickoff event should meet these goals:

- publicly announce the campaign and its goals and objectives,
- explain how and why the goals and objectives were selected,
- introduce campaign leadership,
- announce the amount already pledged,
- build interest among constituents and the media, and
- celebrate the institution's past and future.

Often black-tie affairs, kickoffs should be closely tailored to the campaign's theme, involve representatives from each target audience, and have a sizzle that says the campaign is something special.

Public phase

After the hoopla and glitz of the kickoff, the campaign enters the public phase. The main role of special events during this time is to support the campaign by raising awareness and building interest that is eventually translated into gifts.

Events are used to call attention to crucial date, important announcements, and special people. They launch regional drives, celebrate milestones, signal the end of portions of the campaign, and acknowledge major gifts.

Victory!

Finally the day comes when you have reached or exceeded the capital campaign goal, and you have the pleasure of planning a celebration. While the type and format of the victory event will be unique to your institution, it should communicate the campaign theme and be a first-class affair, the nicest you can afford.

The victory event is the time to say a public thank you to the donors, volunteers, workers, and media who made the campaign a success. A victory event should accomplish the following:

- feature and thank the campaign leaders,
- recognize and thank major donors,
- thank volunteers and workers,
- restate the campaign's purpose,
- provide an update on the progress of other campaign projects such as building construction, and
- lay the foundation for continued giving and involvement.

In addition to a large victory event, you may also want to hold smaller, more personal celebrations for selected groups such as top donors, volunteer leaders, and faculty and staff.

• • •

Independent Planners Can Get the Job Done

A capital campaign kickoff, a founder's day observance, an anniversary open house, a three-day alumni board meeting, and commencement stand between your staff and the end of the academic year. Wouldn't it be nice if you could find another planner to help? You can by contracting with an independent special events planner.

Independent planners offer a wide range of services and will handle everything from conceiving and developing an entire event to simply implementing plans you've already made. Many campuses turn large, time-consuming projects such as auctions, anniversary celebrations, and capital campaign events over to independent planners in order to free staff for managing their regular schedule of events.

Professional event planners may work for large companies or may be one-person operations. Networking with other planners may be the most reliable way to find an independent contractor, check public relations agencies, or look in the Yellow Pages under "meeting planners," "caterers," or "consultants." Large hotels or the local convention and visitors bureau may also be able to give you referrals. If you need help with a technical aspect of an event, independents also may be the answer. Often, independent planners specialize in specific types of events such as social or corporate entertaining, educational conferences, festivals, parades, shopping-mall openings, or political campaigns. You will even find specialists who work in niches such as staging, lighting, or choreography, who provide indoor fireworks, or who create amazing audiovisual presentations.

NOTES

NOTES

NOTES

NOTES

NOTES

NOTES